**Congressional
Research
Service**

Navy DDG-51 and DDG-1000 Destroyer Programs: Background and Issues for Congress

Ronald O'Rourke
Specialist in Naval Affairs

February 4, 2014

Congressional Research Service

7-5700

www.crs.gov

RL32109

Summary

The Navy's FY2014 budget submission called for procuring nine Arleigh Burke (DDG-51) class destroyers in FY2014-FY2018, in annual quantities of 1-2-2-2-2. The three DDG-51s scheduled for procurement in FY2014-FY2015, and the first of the two scheduled for procurement in FY2016, are to be of the current Flight IIA design. The Navy wants to begin procuring a new version of the DDG-51 design, called the Flight III design, starting with the second of the two ships scheduled for procurement in FY2016. The four DDG-51s scheduled for procurement in FY2017-FY2018 are also to be of the Flight III design. The Flight III design is to feature a new and more capable radar called the Air and Missile Defense Radar (AMDR).

The Navy's proposed FY2014 budget requested $1,615.6 million to complete the procurement funding for the one DDG-51 requested for procurement in FY2014. The Navy estimated the total procurement cost of this ship at $1,729.7 million, and the ship had received $114.1 million in prior-year advance procurement (AP) funding. The FY2014 budget also requested $388.6 million in AP funding for DDG-51s to be procured in future fiscal years. The Navy's proposed FY2014 budget also requested $231.7 million in procurement funding to help complete procurement costs for three Zumwalt (DDG-1000) class destroyers procured in FY2007-FY2009, and $240.1 million in research and development funding for the AMDR.

As part of its action on the Navy's FY2013 budget, Congress granted the Navy authority to use a multiyear procurement (MYP) contract for DDG-51s to be procured FY2013-FY2017. The Navy awarded the contract on June 3, 2013. The Navy plans to use an engineering change proposal (ECP) to shift from the Flight IIA design to the Flight III design during this MYP contract. If the Flight III design is not ready to support the procurement of the first Flight III ship in FY2016, the Navy can delay issuing the ECP and shift the start of Flight III procurement to FY2017 or FY2018.

As part of its action on the Navy's FY2013 budget, Congress funded the procurement of three Arleigh Burke (DDG-51) class destroyers, or one more than the two that the Navy had requested for FY2013. Following the March 1, 2013, sequester on Department of Defense (DOD) funding, the Navy indicated that additional funding would be need to be appropriated for the ship to make the ship executable.

Potential FY2013 issues for Congress concerning destroyer procurement include the following:

- the impact on the DDG-51 and DDG-100 programs of the March 1, 2013, sequester on FY2013 funding and unobligated prior-year funding for the programs, including in particular the impact on the executability of the third DDG-51 procured in FY2013;

- a shortfall in cruisers-destroyers that is projected for certain future years;

- whether the Flight III DDG-51 would have sufficient air and missile capability to adequately perform future air and missile defense missions;

- cost, schedule, and technical risk in the Flight III DDG-51 program;

- whether the Flight III DDG-51 design would have sufficient growth margin for a projected 35- or 40-year service life;

- issues raised in a January 2014 report from DOD's Director of Operational Testing and Evaluation (DOT&E); and

- the lack of an announced Navy roadmap for accomplishing three things in the cruiser-destroyer force: restoring ship growth margins; introducing large numbers of ships with integrated electric drive systems or other technologies that could provide ample electrical power for supporting future electrically powered weapons (such as high-power solid state lasers); and introducing technologies (such as those for substantially reducing ship crew size) for substantially reducing ship operating and support (O&S) costs.

Contents

Figures

Tables

Appendixes

Contacts

Introduction

This report presents background information and potential oversight issues for Congress on the Navy's Arleigh Burke (DDG-51) and Zumwalt (DDG-1000) class destroyer programs. The Navy's proposed FY2014 budget requested funding for the procurement of one DDG-51. Decisions that Congress makes concerning these programs could substantially affect Navy capabilities and funding requirements, and the U.S. shipbuilding industrial base.

Background

DDG-51 Program

General

The DDG-51 program was initiated in the late 1970s.[1] The DDG-51 (**Figure 1**) is a multi-mission destroyer with an emphasis on air defense (which the Navy refers as anti-air warfare, or AAW) and blue-water (mid-ocean) operations. DDG-51s, like the Navy's 22 Ticonderoga (CG-47) class cruisers,[2] are equipped with the Aegis combat system, an integrated ship combat system named for the mythological shield that defended Zeus. CG-47s and DDG-51s consequently are often referred to as Aegis cruisers and Aegis destroyers, respectively, or collectively as Aegis ships. The Aegis system has been updated several times over the years. Existing DDG-51s (and also some CG-47s) are being modified to receive an additional capability for ballistic missile defense (BMD) operations.[3]

The first DDG-51 was procured in FY1985. A total of 69 have been procured through FY2013, including 62 in FY1985-FY2005, none during the four-year period FY2006-FY2009, one in FY2010, two in FY2011, one in FY2012, and three in FY2013. The first DDG-51 entered service in 1991, and a total of 62 were in service as of the end of FY2012. DDG-51s are built by General Dynamics Bath Iron Works (GD/BIW) of Bath, ME, and Ingalls Shipbuilding of Pascagoula, MS, a division of Huntington Ingalls Industries (HII).

The DDG-51 design has been modified over time. The first 28 DDG-51s (i.e., DDGs 51 through 78) are called Flight I/II DDG-51s. Subsequent ships in the class (i.e., DDGs 79 and higher) are referred to as Flight IIA DDG-51s. The Flight IIA design, first procured in FY1994, implemented a significant design change that included, among other things, the addition of a helicopter hangar.

---

[1] The program was initiated with the aim of developing a surface combatant to replace older destroyers and cruisers that were projected to retire in the 1990s. The DDG-51 was conceived as an affordable complement to the Navy's Ticonderoga (CG-47) class Aegis cruisers.

[2] A total of 27 CG-47s were procured for the Navy between FY1978 and FY1988; the ships entered service between 1983 and 1994. The first five, which were built to an earlier technical standard, were judged by the Navy to be too expensive to modernize and were removed from service in 2004-2005.

[3] The modification for BMD operations includes, among other things, the addition of a new software program for the Aegis combat system and the arming of the ship with the SM-3, a version of the Navy's Standard Missile that is designed for BMD operations. For more on Navy BMD programs, CRS Report RL33745, *Navy Aegis Ballistic Missile Defense (BMD) Program: Background and Issues for Congress*, by Ronald O'Rourke.

The Flight IIA design has a full load displacement of about 9,500 tons, which is similar to that of the CG-47.

Figure 1. DDG-51 Class Destroyer

The Navy's FY2013 30-year (FY2013-FY2042) shipbuilding plan assumes a 35-year service life for Flight I/II DDG-51s and a 40-year service life for Flight IIA DDG-51s. The Navy is implementing a program for modernizing all DDG-51s (and CG-47s) so as to maintain their mission and cost effectiveness out to the end of their projected service lives.[4]

Older CRS reports provide additional historical and background information on the DDG-51 program.[5]

Resumption of Flight IIA DDG-51 Procurement in FY2010

The Navy in July 2008 announced that it wanted to end procurement of DDG-1000 destroyers (see "DDG-1000 Program" below) and resume procurement of Flight IIA DDG-51s. The

---

[4] For more on this program, see CRS Report RS22595, *Navy Aegis Cruiser and Destroyer Modernization: Background and Issues for Congress*, by Ronald O'Rourke.

[5] See CRS Report 94-343, *Navy DDG-51 Destroyer Procurement Rate: Issues and Options for Congress*, by Ronald O'Rourke (April 25, 1994; out of print and available directly from the author), and CRS Report 80-205, *The Navy's Proposed Arleigh Burke (DDG-51) Class Guided Missile Destroyer Program: A Comparison With An Equal-Cost Force Of Ticonderoga (CG-47) Class Guided Missile Destroyers*, by Ronald O'Rourke (November 21, 1984; out of print and available directly from the author).

---

announcement represented a major change in Navy planning: prior to the announcement, the Navy for years had strongly supported ending DDG-51 procurement permanently in FY2005 and proceeding with procurement of DDG-1000 destroyers.[6] The Navy's FY2010 budget, submitted in May 2009, reflected the Navy's July 2008 change in plans: the budget proposed truncating DDG-1000 procurement to the three ships that had been procured in FY2007 and FY2009, and resuming procurement of Flight IIA DDG-51s. Congress, as part of its action on the FY2010 defense budget, supported the proposal.[7]

Procurement of First Flight III DDG-51 Planned for FY2016

The Navy's FY2011 budget, submitted in February 2010, proposed another major change in Navy plans—terminating a planned cruiser called the CG(X) in favor of procuring an improved version of the DDG-51 called the Flight III version.[8] Rather than starting to procure CG(X)s around FY2017, Navy plans call for procuring the first Flight III DDG-51 in FY2016.

Compared to the Flight IIA DDG-51 design, the Flight III design is to feature a new and more capable radar called the Air and Missile Defense Radar (AMDR). The version of the AMDR to be carried by the Flight III DDG-51 is smaller and less powerful than the one envisaged for the CG(X): the Flight III DDG-51's AMDR is to have a diameter of 14 feet, while the AMDR envisaged for the CG(X) would have had a substantially larger diameter.[9]

---

[6] The Navy announced this change in its plans at a July 31, 2008, hearing before the Seapower and Expeditionary Forces subcommittee of the House Armed Services Committee. In explaining their proposed change in plans, Navy officials cited a reassessment of threats that Navy forces are likely to face in coming years. As a result of this reassessment, Navy officials stated, the service decided that destroyer procurement over the next several years should emphasize three mission capabilities—area-defense AAW, BMD, and open-ocean ASW. Navy officials also stated that they want to maximize the number of destroyers that can be procured over the next several years within budget constraints. Navy officials stated that DDG-51s can provide the area-defense AAW, BMD, and open-ocean ASW capabilities that the Navy wants to emphasize, and that while the DDG-1000 design could also be configured to provide these capabilities, the Navy could procure more DDG-51s than reconfigured DDG-1000s over the next several years for the same total amount of funding. In addition, the Navy by 2008-2009 no longer appeared committed to the idea of reusing the DDG-1000 hull as the basis for the Navy's planned CG(X) cruiser. If the Navy had remained committed to that idea, it might have served as a reason for continuing DDG-1000 procurement.

[7] The FY2010 budget funded the procurement of one DDG-51, provided advance procurement funding for two DDG-51s the Navy wants to procure in FY2011, completed the procurement funding for the third DDG-1000 (which was authorized but only partially funded in FY2009), and provided no funding for procuring additional DDG-1000s.

[8] The Navy stated that its desire to terminate the CG(X) program was "driven by affordability considerations." (Department of the Navy, Office of Budget, *Highlights of the Department of the Navy FY 2011 Budget*, February 2010, p. 5-7.) For more on the CG(X) program and its termination in favor of procuring Flight III DDG-51s, see **Appendix B**.

[9] Government Accountability Office, *Arleigh Burke Destroyers[:] Additional Analysis and Oversight Required to Support the Navy's Future Surface Combatant Plans*, GAO-12-113, January 2012, pp. 31 and 42. See also Zachary M. Peterson, "DDG-51 With Enhanced Radar in FY-16, Design Work To Begin Soon," *Inside the Navy*, February 8, 2010; Amy Butler, "STSS Prompts Shift in CG(X) Plans," *Aerospace Daily & Defense Report*, December 11, 2010: 1-2; "[Interview With] Vice Adm. Barry McCullough," *Defense News*, November 9, 2009: 38.

The written testimony of the Chief of Naval Operations (CNO) before the House Armed Services Committee on February 16, 2012, and before the Defense subcommittee of the House Appropriations Committee on March 1, 2012, stated that the Flight III design would use an all-electric propulsion system, in contrast to the mechanical propulsion system used on the Flight IIA design and other Navy surface combatants. (See, for example, Statement of Admiral Jonathan Greenert, Chief of Naval Operations, Before the House Armed Services Committee [hearing] on FY2013 Department of the Navy Posture, February 16, 2012, which stated on page 10: "Our Lewis and Clark class supply ships now employ an all-electric propulsion system, as will our new Zumwalt and Flight III Arleigh Burke class destroyers (DDG).") The written testimony of the CNO before the Defense subcommittee of the Senate Appropriations Committee on March 7, 2012, and before the Senate Armed Services Committee on March 15, 2012, omitted the reference to the (continued...)

On July 24, 2012, Frank Kendall, the Under Secretary of Defense for Acquisition, Technology and Logistics (or USD ATL—the acquisition executive for the Department of Defense), designated the DDG-51 program as an Acquisition Category (ACAT) 1D program, meaning that he (rather than the Secretary of the Navy or the Navy's acquisition executive) will act as the Milestone Decision Authority (MDA) for the DDG-51 program.

As mentioned earlier, the two DDG-51s that the Navy wants to procure in FY2016 include the final Flight IIA DDG-51 and the first Flight III DDG-51. The combined cost for these two ships shown in the Navy's FY2013 budget submission suggests that the Navy estimates the procurement cost of the first Flight III DDG-51 at roughly $2.3 billion. The FY2014 budget estimates that the two Flight III DDG-51s scheduled for procurement in FY2017 would cost an average of about $1.9 billion each.

Multiyear Procurement (MYP) in FY2013-FY2017

As part of its action on the Navy's FY2013 budget, Congress granted the Navy authority to use a multiyear procurement (MYP) contract for DDG-51s to be procured FY2013-FY2017.[10] The Navy awarded the contract on June 3, 2013.[11] The Navy plans to use an engineering change proposal (ECP) to shift from the Flight IIA design to the Flight III design during this MYP contract. If the Flight III design is not ready to support the procurement of the first Flight III ship in FY2016, the Navy can delay issuing the ECP and shift the start of Flight III procurement to FY2017 or FY2018.

DDG-1000 Program

The DDG-1000 program was initiated in the early 1990s.[12] The DDG-1000 is a multi-mission destroyer with an emphasis on naval surface fire support (NSFS) and operations in littoral (i.e., near-shore) waters. The DDG-1000 is intended to replace, in a technologically more modern form, the large-caliber naval gun fire capability that the Navy lost when it retired its Iowa-class battleships in the early 1990s,[13] to improve the Navy's general capabilities for operating in defended littoral waters, and to introduce several new technologies that would be available for use on future Navy ships. The DDG-1000 was also intended to serve as the basis for the Navy's now-canceled CG(X) cruiser.

(...continued)

Flight III DDG-51 being equipped with an all-electric propulsion system. In response to a question from CRS about the change in the testimony, the Navy informed CRS on March 15, 2012, that the statement in the earlier testimony was an error, and that the Flight III DDG-51 will likely not be equipped with an all-electric propulsion system.

[10] For more on MYP contracts, see CRS Report R41909, *Multiyear Procurement (MYP) and Block Buy Contracting in Defense Acquisition: Background and Issues for Congress*, by Ronald O'Rourke and Moshe Schwartz.

[11] "DDG 51 Multiyear Procurement Contract Awarded," *Navy News Service*, June 3, 2013, accessed online July 1, 2013, at http://www.navy mil/submit/display.asp?story_id=74583. See also Mike McCarthy, "Navy Awards Multi-Year Contracts For Destroyers," *Defense Daily*, June 4, 2013: 1.

[12] The program was originally designated DD-21, which meant destroyer for the 21st Century. In November 2001, the program was restructured and renamed DD(X), meaning a destroyer whose design was in development. In April 2006, the program's name was changed again, to DDG-1000, meaning a guided missile destroyer with the hull number 1000.

[13] The Navy in the 1980s reactivated and modernized four Iowa (BB-61) class battleships that were originally built during World War II. The ships reentered service between 1982 and 1988 and were removed from service between 1990 and 1992.

The DDG-1000 is to have a reduced-size crew of 142 sailors (compared to roughly 300 on the Navy's Aegis destroyers and cruisers) so as to reduce its operating and support (O&S) costs. The ship incorporates a significant number of new technologies, including an integrated electric-drive propulsion system[14] and automation technologies enabling its reduced-sized crew.

With an estimated full load displacement of 15,482 tons, the DDG-1000 design is roughly 63% larger than the Navy's current 9,500-ton Aegis cruisers and destroyers, and larger than any Navy destroyer or cruiser since the nuclear-powered cruiser *Long Beach* (CGN-9), which was procured in FY1957.

The first two DDG-1000s were procured in FY2007 and split-funded (i.e., funded with two-year incremental funding) in FY2007-FY2008; the Navy's FY2013 budget submission estimates their combined procurement cost at $7,795.2 million. The third DDG-1000 was procured in FY2009 and split-funded in FY2009-FY2010; the Navy's FY2013 budget submission estimates its procurement cost at $3,674.9 million.

The estimated combined procurement cost for all three ships in the FY2014 budget is $11,618.4 million, compared to $11,470.1 million in the FY2013 budget, $11,308.8 million shown in the FY2012 budget, and $9,993.3 million in the FY2011 budget.

All three ships are to be built at GD/BIW, with some portions of each ship being built by Ingalls Shipbuilding for delivery to GD/BIW. Raytheon is the prime contractor for the DDG-1000's combat system (its collection of sensors, computers, related software, displays, and weapon launchers). The Navy awarded GD/BIW the contract for the construction of the second and third DDG-1000s on September 15, 2011.[15]

For additional background information on the DDG-1000 program, see **Appendix A**.

Projected Shortfall in Cruisers and Destroyers

A January 2013 Navy report to Congress establishes a cruiser-destroyer force-level objective of 88 ships.[16] The FY2014 30-year (FY2014-FY2043) shipbuilding plan does not contain enough destroyers to maintain a force of 88 cruisers and destroyers consistently over the long run. As shown in **Table 1**, the Navy projects that implementing the FY2014 30-year shipbuilding plan would result in a cruiser-destroyer force that remains below 88 ships for more than half of the 30-year period, and that bottoms out in FY2015 at 78 ships—10 ships, or about 11% below the required figure of about 88 ships.

---

[14] For more on integrated electric-drive technology, see CRS Report RL30622, *Electric-Drive Propulsion for U.S. Navy Ships: Background and Issues for Congress*, by Ronald O'Rourke.

[15] See, for example, Mike McCarthy, "Navy Awards Contract for DDG-1000s," *Defense Daily*, September 16, 2011: 3-4.

[16] Department of the Navy, *Report to Congress [on] Navy Combatant Vessel Force Structure Requirement*, January 2013, 3 pp. The cover letters for the report were dated January 31, 2013. The previous cruiser-destroyer force-level objective—set forth in the Navy's FY2013 30-year (FY2013-FY2042) shipbuilding plan—was for a force of about 90 ships. Before that, an April 2011 report to Congress on naval force structure and ballistic missile defense (U.S. Navy, Office of the Chief of Naval Operations, Director of Strategy and Policy (N51), *Report to Congress On Naval Force Structure and Missile Defense*, April 2011, 12 pp.) had increased the cruiser-destroyer force-level goal from 88 ships to 94 ships. For more on Navy ship force-level goals, see CRS Report RL32665, *Navy Force Structure and Shipbuilding Plans: Background and Issues for Congress*, by Ronald O'Rourke.

The Navy's FY2013 budget submission proposed early retirements in FY2013 and FY2014 for a total of seven CG-47s. Congress, as part of its action on the Navy's FY2013 budget, instructed the Navy to keep the seven CG-47s in service, and provided funding in a newly established Ship Modernization, Operations and Sustainment Fund (SMOSF),[17] for the continued operation and support of these seven ships (and also two amphibious ships that were proposed for early retirements) in FY2013 and FY2014. The decrease shown in **Table 1** from 85 cruisers and destroyers in FY2014 to 78 cruisers and destroyers in FY2015 suggests that the Navy now plans early retirements in FY2015 for seven CG-47s (although not necessarily the same CG-47s that were proposed for early retirement under the Navy proposed FY2013 budget).

Table 1. Projected Cruiser-Destroyer Shortfall

As shown in Navy's FY2014 30-Year Shipbuilding Plan

Fiscal year	Projected number of cruisers and destroyers	Shortfall relative to 88-ship goal, shown as a negative	
		Number of ships	Percent
14	85	-3	-3%
15	78	-10	-11%
16	82	-6	-7%
17	83	-5	-6%
18	84	-4	-5%
19	86	-2	-2%
20	87	-1	-1%
21	88		
22	87	-1	-1%
23	87	-1	-1%
24	89		
25	88		
26	89		
27	91		
28	90		
29	88		
30	86	-2	-2%
31	82	-6	-7%
32	81	-7	-8%
33	81	-7	-8%
34	80	-8	-9%
35	82	-6	-7%
36	84	-4	-5%

---

[17] The fund was established by Section 8103 of Division C (the FY2013 DOD appropriations act) of the Consolidated and Further Continuing Appropriations Act, 2013 (H.R. 933/P.L. 113-6 of March 26, 2013).

Fiscal year	Projected number of cruisers and destroyers	Shortfall relative to 88-ship goal, shown as a negative	
		Number of ships	Percent
37	86	-2	-2%
38	88		
39	90		
40	90		
41	90		
42	88		
43	88		

Source: Table prepared by CRS based on Navy's FY2014-FY2043 30-year shipbuilding plan. Percentage figures rounded to nearest percent.

Surface Combatant Construction Industrial Base

All cruisers, destroyers, and frigates procured since FY1985 have been built at General Dynamics' Bath Iron Works (GD/BIW) shipyard of Bath, ME, and Ingalls Shipbuilding of Pascagoula, MS, a division of Huntington Ingalls Industries (HII).[18] Both yards have long histories of building larger surface combatants. Construction of Navy surface combatants in recent years has accounted for virtually all of GD/BIW's ship-construction work and for a significant share of Ingalls' ship-construction work. (Ingalls also builds amphibious ships for the Navy.) Navy surface combatants are overhauled, repaired, and modernized at GD/BIW, Ingalls, other private-sector U.S. shipyards, and government-operated naval shipyards (NSYs).

Lockheed Martin and Raytheon are generally considered the two leading Navy surface combatant radar makers and combat system integrators. Northrop Grumman is a third potential maker of Navy surface combatant radars. Lockheed is the lead contractor for the DDG-51 combat system (the Aegis system), while Raytheon is the lead contractor for the DDG-1000 combat system, the core of which is called the Total Ship Computing Environment Infrastructure (TSCE-I). Lockheed has a share of the DDG-1000 combat system, and Raytheon has a share of the DDG-51 combat system. Lockheed, Raytheon, and Northrop competed to be the maker of the AMDR to be carried by the Flight III DDG-51. On October 10, 2013, the Navy announced that it had selected Raytheon to be the maker of the AMDR.

The surface combatant construction industrial base also includes hundreds of additional firms that supply materials and components. The financial health of Navy shipbuilding supplier firms has been a matter of concern in recent years, particularly since some of them are the sole sources for what they make for Navy surface combatants.

FY2014 Funding Request

The Navy's proposed FY2014 budget requested $1,615.6 million to complete the procurement funding for the one DDG-51 requested for procurement in FY2014. The Navy estimated the total

---

[18] HII was previously owned by Northrop Grumman, during which time it was known as Northrop Grumman Shipbuilding.

procurement cost of this ship at $1,729.7 million, and the ship has received $114.1 million in prior-year advance procurement (AP) funding. The FY2014 budget also requested $388.6 million in AP funding for DDG-51s to be procured in future fiscal years. The Navy's proposed FY2014 budget also requested $231.7 million in procurement funding to help complete procurement costs for three Zumwalt (DDG-1000) class destroyers procured in FY2007-FY2009, and $240.1 million in research and development funding for the AMDR. The funding request for the AMDR is contained in the Navy's research and development account in Project 3186 ("Air and Missile Defense Radar") of Program Element (PE) 0604501N ("Advanced Above Water Sensors").

Issues for Congress

Impact of March 1, 2013, Sequester on FY2013 Funding

One issue for Congress concerns the impact on the DDG-51 and DDG-1000 programs of the March 1, 2013, sequester on FY2013 funding (and unobligated prior-year funding) for the programs. The Department of Defense's (DOD's) June 2013 report to Congress on the March 1, 2013, sequester states that the sequester reduced FY2013 and prior-year procurement funding for the DDG-51 program by $541.2 million and FY2013 and prior-year procurement funding for the DDG-1000 program by $70.3 million.[19]

DDG-51 Program

A particular issue regarding the impact of the March 1, 2013, sequester concerns the executability (i.e., the Navy's ability to go ahead with the construction) of the third DDG-51 procured in FY2013. This ship is to be the 10th ship in the DDG-51 multiyear procurement (MYP) contract for FY2013-FY2017 that was awarded on June 3, 2013. In its prepared statement for a May 8, 2013, hearing on Navy shipbuilding programs before the Seapower subcommittee of the Senate Armed Services Committee, the Navy stated that "The Department [of the Navy]'s objective is to procure the tenth DDG 51 in the MYP; however, we will first need to resolve funding shortfalls resulting from the Fiscal Year 2013 sequestration reductions."[20] In the discussion portion of the hearing, Sean Stackley, the Assistant Secretary of the Navy for Research, Development and Acquisition (i.e., the Navy's acquisition executive), testified that as a result of the March 1, 2013, sequester, there is an approximately $300 million funding shortfall in the DDG-51 program that creates a problem for executing the third DDG-51 that was funded in FY2013.[21] Stackley stated

---

[19] *Department of Defense Report on the Joint Committee Sequestration for Fiscal Year 2013*, June 2013, p. 36A (pdf page 86 of 438).

[20] Statement of The Honorable Sean J. Stackley, Assistant Secretary of the Navy (Research, Development and Acquisition) and Vice Admiral Allen G. Myers, Deputy Chief of Naval Operations for Integration of Capabilities and Resources and Vice Admiral Kevin M. McCoy, Commander, Naval Sea Systems Command, Before the Subcommittee on Seapower of the Senate Armed Services Committee on Department of the Navy Shipbuilding Programs, May 8, 2013, p. 11.

[21] Transcript of hearing. Stackley, citing a figure somewhat different from the $541.2 million figure in DOD's June 2013 report to Congress on the March 1, 2013, sequester, testified that the sequester created an approximately $560 million funding shortfall in the DDG-51 program, and that the Navy has been able to identify about $260 million in funding offsets to apply to the shortfall, leaving a shortfall of about $300 million.

that the Navy is ready to work with Congress to address this issue, and that the ship is treated as an option in the DDG-51 MYP contract.[22]

The suggestion from the testimony is that if Congress were to address the funding shortfall for the DDG-51 program this year, either through its action on the Navy's proposed FY2014 budget or in some other way, the ship could be added to the MYP contract by exercising the contract's option for the ship. If that were to happen this year, it would not substantially affect the schedule for building this ship, because the Navy from the start has anticipated building the ship on a schedule consistent with what would be expected for a ship funded in FY2014. In other words, for construction scheduling purposes, the Navy from the start has anticipated treating the ship like a "second FY2014 DDG-51" rather than a third FY2013 DDG-51.

DDG-1000 Program

Regarding the impact of the March 1, 2013, sequester on the DDG-1000 program, Sean Stackley, the Assistant Secretary of the Navy for Research, Development and Acquisition (i.e., the Navy's acquisition executive), testified at a May 8, 2013, hearing on Navy shipbuilding programs before the Seapower subcommittee of the Senate Armed Services Committee that the DDG-1000 program has

> a lot of developmental activities that are going along side by side with the ship construction. And so we're impacted in terms of development associated with the lead ship and also procurement associated with the lead ship. So we're very concerned that we don't have the ability to make up that reduction.
>
> We have limitations in terms of our reprogramming authority. We have limited assets under a sequestration in order to be able to offer up an asset to backfill. So we are stuck in '13 with that reduction. And we don't have the ability to fix it in '14. And the budget request, in fact, did not anticipate having to backfill '13 sequestration.[23]

A June 24, 2013, press report stated:

> The $80 million in shipbuilding and research and development funds that sequestration took out of the DDG-1000 program in fiscal year 2013 may delay construction of the third ship in the class and puts at risk certification for the ship class's new missile system....
>
> Sequestration has cut funding for the ship class by $70 million in the shipbuilding account and by $10 million in the research, development, test and evaluation account, NAVSEA [Naval Sea Systems Command] spokesman Lt. Kurt Larson told *Inside the Navy*....
>
> As a result of the cuts, procurement for DDG-1002 is being "rephased to later years," and 10 of the 15 remaining Long-Range Land Attack Projectile guided flight tests are at risk.[24]

---

[22] Transcript of hearing.

[23] Transcript of hearing.

[24] Megan Eckstein, "$80 Million Sequestration Cut Slows DDG-1002 Buy, Testing (Updated)," *Inside the Navy*, June 24, 2013.

Projected Cruiser-Destroyer Shortfall

Another issue for Congress is the shortfall in cruisers-destroyers projected for certain future years that is shown in **Table 1**. Options for mitigating this projected shortfall include adding DDG-51s to the Navy's shipbuilding plan and extending the service lives of some Flight I/II DDG-51s to 40 or 45 years (i.e., 5 or 10 years beyond their currently planned 35-year service lives). Extending the service lives of Flight I/II DDG-51s could require increasing, perhaps soon, funding levels for the maintenance of these ships, to help ensure they would remain in good enough shape to eventually have their lives extended for another 5 or 10 years. This additional maintenance funding would be on top of funding that the Navy has already programmed to help ensure that these ships can remain in service to the end of their currently planned 35-year lives. The potential need to increase maintenance funding soon could make the question of whether to extend the lives of these ships a potentially near-term issue for policymakers.

Flight III DDG-51: Adequacy of AAW and BMD Capability

Another issue for Congress is whether the Flight III DDG-51 would have sufficient AAW and BMD capability to adequately perform future AAW and BMD missions. The Flight III DDG-51 would have more AAW and BMD capability than the current DDG-51 design, but less AAW and BMD capability than was envisioned for the CG(X) cruiser, in large part because the Flight III DDG-51 would be equipped with a 14-foot-diameter version of the AMDR that would have more sensitivity than the SPY-1 radar on Flight IIA DDG-51s, but less sensitivity than the substantially larger version of the AMDR that was envisioned for the CG(X). The CG(X) also may have had more missile-launch tubes than the Flight III DDG-51.

The Navy argues that while the version of the AMDR on the Flight III DDG-51 will have less sensitivity than the larger version of the AMDR envisioned for the CG(X), the version of the AMDR on the Flight III DDG-51 will provide sufficient AAW and BMD capability to address future air and missile threats. A March 2013 Government Accountability Office (GAO) report assessing selected DOD acquisition programs stated:

> The Navy plans to install a 14-foot variant of AMDR on Flight III DDG 51s starting in 2019. According to draft AMDR documents, a 14-foot radar is needed to meet threshold requirements, but an over 20-foot radar is required to fully meet the Navy's desired integrated air and missile defense needs. However, the shipyards and the Navy have determined that a 14-foot active radar is the largest that can be accommodated within the existing DDG 51 deckhouse. Navy officials stated that AMDR is being developed as a scalable design but a new ship would be required to host a larger version of AMDR....

> The X-band portion of AMDR will be comprised of an upgraded version of an existing rotating radar (SPQ-9B), instead of the new design initially planned. The new radar will instead be developed as a separate program at a later date and integrated with the 13th AMDR unit. According to the Navy, the SPQ-9B radar fits better within the Flight III DDG 51's sea frame and expected power and cooling. While program officials state that the upgraded SPQ-9B radar will have capabilities equal to the new design for current anti-air warfare threats, it will not perform as well against future threats.[25]

---

[25] Government Accountability Office, *Defense Acquisitions[:] Assessments of Selected Weapon Programs*, GAO-13-294SP, March 2013, p. 46.

Flight III DDG-51: Cost, Technical, and Schedule Risk

Another issue for Congress concerns cost, technical, and schedule risk for the Flight III DDG-51. Some observers have expressed concern about the Navy's ability to complete development of the AMDR and deliver the first AMDR to the shipyard in time to support the construction schedule for a first Flight III DDG-51 procured in FY2016. The Navy could respond to a delay in the development of the AMDR by shifting the procurement of the first Flight III DDG-51 to FY2017 or a later year, while continuing to procure Flight IIA DDG-51s. (The MYP that the Navy has awarded for FY2013-FY2017 is structured to accommodate such a shift, should it become necessary.) Some observers have also expressed concern about the potential procurement cost of the Flight III DDG-51 design.

October 2013 CBO Report

An October 2013 Congressional Budget Office (CBO) report on the cost of the Navy's shipbuilding programs stated:

> Adding the AMDR [to the DDG-51 design] so that it could operate effectively would require increasing the amount of electrical power and cooling available on a Flight III. With those changes and associated increases in the ship's displacement, a DDG-51 Flight III destroyer would cost about $300 million, or about 20 percent, more than a new Flight IIA destroyer, CBO estimates. Thus, the average cost per ship [for Flight III DDG-51s] would be $1.9 billion....
>
> CBO's estimate of the costs of the DDG Flight IIA and Flight III ships to be purchased in the future is less than it was last year. Most of the decrease for the Flight III can be attributed to updated information on the cost of incorporating the AMDR into the Flight III configuration. The cost of the AMDR itself, according to the Navy, has declined steadily through the development program, and the Department of Defense's Cost Analysis and Program Evaluation (CAPE) office concurs in the reduced estimate. The Navy decreased its estimate for the average price of a DDG-51 Flight III ship from $2.2 billion in the 2013 plan to $1.8 billion in the 2014 plan, primarily as a result of the reduced cost of the AMDR. CBO reduced its estimate by a similar amount. Considerable uncertainty remains in the DDG-51 Flight III program, however. Costs could be higher or lower than CBO's estimate, depending on how well the restart of the DDG-51 program goes, on the eventual cost and complexity of the AMDR, and on associated changes in the ship's design to integrate the new radar.[26]

March 2013 GAO Report

A March 2013 Government Accountability Office (GAO) report assessing selected DOD acquisition programs stated the following in its assessment of the DDG-51 program: "To date, the Navy has identified the AMDR as the only major new technology for Flight III, but more technologies are under consideration. The integration of AMDR will require changes to the power architecture."[27] Regarding the AMDR specifically, the report stated:

---

[26] Congressional Budget Office, *An Analysis of the Navy's Fiscal Year 2014 Shipbuilding Plan*, October 2013, pp. 25, 27.

[27] Government Accountability Office, *Defense Acquisitions[:] Assessments of Selected Weapon Programs*, GAO-13-294SP, March 2013, p. 139.

According to the program office, all four of AMDR's critical technologies are approaching maturity. Testing on scaled-down prototypes was conducted with the three contractors during the summer of 2012 as part of their technology development contracts. The program previously had six critical technologies; two are still tested but no longer considered critical.

According to the program, two technologies previously identified as the most challenging—digital-beam-forming and transmit-receive modules—have been demonstrated in a relevant environment. Program officials stated that no significant issues were identified at the preliminary design review with the digital beamforming technology necessary for AMDR's simultaneous air and ballistic missile defense mission. The transmit-receive modules—the individual radiating elements key to transmitting and receiving electromagnetic signals—are a new design which utilizes gallium nitride semiconductor technology instead of the legacy gallium arsenide technology. The new technology has the potential to provide higher efficiency with smaller power and cooling demands. While gallium nitride has never been used in a radar as large as AMDR, and long-term reliability and performance of this newer material is unknown, the preliminary design reviews concluded that the contractors have demonstrated good power and efficiency thus far. The other two critical technologies, related to software and digital receivers and exciters, were also successfully demonstrated.

According to program officials, software development for AMDR will require a significant effort. A series of software builds are expected to deliver approximately 1 million lines of code, with additional testing assets also being developed. Software will be designed to apply open system approaches to commercial, off-the-shelf hardware. Integration with the SPQ-9B radar, and later the AMDR-X radar, will require further software development.[28]

Flight III DDG-51: Growth Margin

Another issue for Congress is whether the Flight III DDG-51 design would have sufficient growth margin for a projected 35- or 40-year service life. A ship's growth margin refers to its capacity for being fitted over time with either additional equipment or newer equipment that is larger, heavier, or more power-intensive than the older equipment it is replacing, so as to preserve the ship's mission effectiveness. Elements of a ship's growth margin include interior space, weight-carrying capacity, electrical power, cooling capacity (to cool equipment), and ability to accept increases in the ship's vertical center of gravity. Navy ship classes are typically designed so that the first ships in the class will be built with a certain amount of growth margin. Over time, some or all of the growth margin in a ship class may be used up by backfitting additional or newer systems onto existing ships in the class, or by building later ships in the class to a modified design that includes additional or newer systems.

Modifying the DDG-51 design over time has used up some of the design's growth margin. The Flight III DDG-51 would in some respects have less of a growth margin than what the Navy would aim to include in a new destroyer design of about the same size. A January 18, 2013, press report stated, "In making decisions about the [Flight III] ship's power, cooling, weight and other margins, [DDG-51 program manager Captain Mark] Vandroff said [in a presentation at a conference on January 15, 2013, that] the Navy wanted to ensure that there was room to grow in the future, to allow for modernization as well as capability upgrades when new weapons such as the electromagnetic railgun enter the fleet. Allowing for growth was balanced with cost, and Vandroff said he thought the program did a great job of coming up with an affordable solution to

---

[28] Government Accountability Office, *Defense Acquisitions[:] Assessments of Selected Weapon Programs*, GAO-13-294SP, March 2013, p. 46.

a leap-ahead capability for the fleet."[29] In his presentation, Vandroff showed a slide comparing the growth margins of the Flight III design to those of Flight IIA DDG-51s procured or scheduled to be procured in FY2010-FY2014; the slide is reproduced below as **Figure 2**.

---

[29] Megan Eckstein, "Flight III DDGs To Cost About $2 Billion, Have Margins For Future Growth," *Inside the Navy*, January 18, 2013.

Figure 2. Navy Briefing Slide on DDG-51 Growth Margins

Flight III DDG-51 Design Compared to Flight IIA DDG-51s

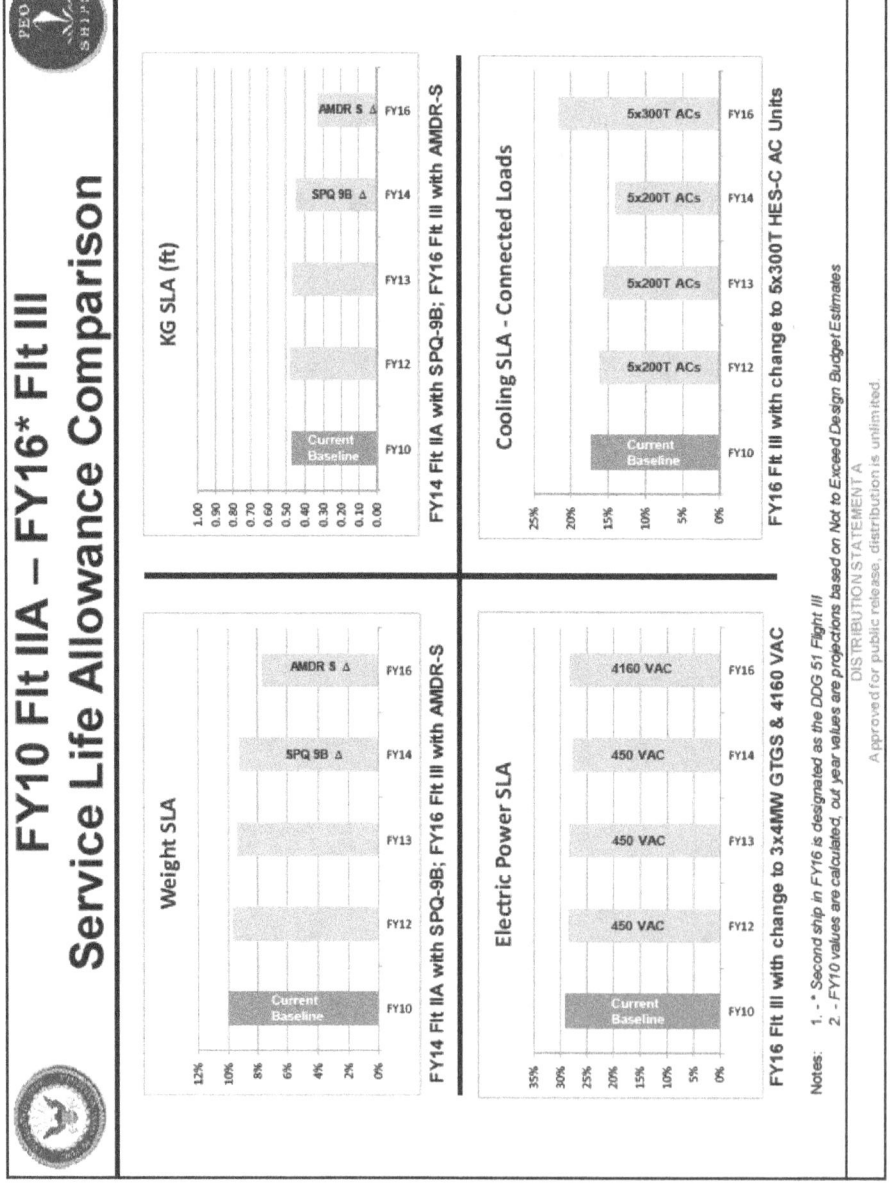

Source: Presentation of Captain Mark Vandroff to Surface Navy Association, January 15-17, 2013; a copy of the slides was provided to CRS by the Navy Office of Legislative Affairs on January 28, 2013.

Note: SLA means service life allowance (i.e., growth margin).

A June 7, 2013, blog post stated:

> The Navy is confident it has enough space, power and cooling onboard the hull of its planned new line of destroyers to accommodate the planned high-powered Air and Missile Defense Radar (AMDR), Capt. Mark Vandroff, Naval Sea Systems Command program manager for the DDG-51 shipbuilding program, told USNI News in an interview on Thursday.
>
> However, the Arleigh Burke-class destroyer (DDG-51) Flight III would be limited in the amount of additional weapons the ship could accommodate—including electromagnetic railguns and high-energy lasers—without removing other capabilities.
>
> "Depending on how heavy that railgun is, could you fit it on a DDG? My answer is what on that DDG are you willing to live without right now?" Vandroff said.
>
> "You wouldn't have the space and weight to put on something very large without something relatively sizable coming off."[30]

Supporters of the Navy's proposal to procure Flight III DDG-51s could argue that the ship's growth margin would be comparable to that of recently procured Flight IIA DDG-51s, and would be adequate because the increase in capability achieved with the Flight III configuration reduces the likelihood that the ship will need much subsequent modification to retain its mission effectiveness over its projected service life. They could also argue that, given technology advances, new systems added to the ship years from now might require no more (and possibly less) space, weight, electrical power, or cooling capacity than the older systems they replace.

Skeptics could argue that there are uncertainties involved in projecting what types of capabilities ships might need to have to remain mission effective over a 35- or 40-year life, and that building expensive new warships with relatively modest growth margins consequently would be imprudent. The Flight III DDG-51's growth margin, they could argue, could make it more likely that the ships would need to be removed from service well before the end of their projected service lives due to an inability to accept modifications needed to preserve their mission effectiveness. Skeptics could argue that it might not be possible to fit the Flight III DDG-51 in the future with a high-power (200 kW to 300 kW) solid state laser (SSL), because the ship would not have enough available electrical power or cooling capacity to support such a weapon. Skeptics could argue that high-power SSLs could be critical to the Navy's ability years from now to affordably counter large numbers of enemy anti-ship cruise missiles (ASCMs) and anti-ship ballistic missiles (ASBMs) that might be fielded by a wealthy and determined adversary. Skeptics could argue that procuring Flight III DDG-51s could delay the point at which high-power SSLs could be introduced into the cruiser-destroyer force, and reduce for many years the portion of the cruiser-destroyer force that could ultimately be backfitted with high-power SSLs. This, skeptics could argue, might result in an approach to AAW and BMD on cruisers and destroyers that might ultimately be unaffordable for the Navy to sustain in a competition against a wealthy and determined adversary.[31]

---

[30] "NAVSEA on Flight III Arleigh Burkes," *USNI News*, June 7, 2013, accessed July 1, 2013, at http://news.usni.org/ 2013/06/07/navsea-on-flight-iii-arleigh-burkes.

[31] For more on potential shipboard lasers, see CRS Report R41526, *Navy Shipboard Lasers for Surface, Air, and Missile Defense: Background and Issues for Congress*, by Ronald O'Rourke.

Flight III DDG-51: Issues Raised in January 2014 DOT&E Report

Another issue for Congress concerns issues raised in a January 2014 report from DOD's Director of Operational Test and Evaluation (DOT&E)—DOT&E's annual report for FY2013. Regarding the Flight III DDG-51 program, the report stated:

Executive Summary

• On May 22, 2013, DOT&E disapproved the Air and Missile Defense Radar (AMDR) Test and Evaluation Master Plan (TEMP) because the proposed operational test approach did not adequately assess the capability of that radar to support the DDG 51 Flight III Destroyer's self-defense mission.

- Safety restrictions preclude realistic testing on manned ships in this region of the battlespace. Consequently, an unmanned test ship equipped with an AMDR and an Aegis DDG 51 Flight III Destroyer Combat System is required for adequate operational testing and assessment of the AMDR and DDG 51 Flight III Destroyer's self-defense capabilities.

- This approach is similar to the Self-Defense Test Ship (SDTS) currently used for testing the self-defense capabilities of ships equipped with Ship Self-Defense System (SSDS)-based combat systems

• On August 9, 2013, DOT&E disapproved the Aegis Modernization TEMP because the proposed operational testing did not provide the credible modeling and simulation (M&S) effort needed to fully assess the DDG 51's combat system self-defense capability, nor a means to validate the M&S (i.e., an unmanned SDTS equipped with an AMDR and the DDG 51 Flight III Combat System)....

Activity

• DOT&E issued two classified memoranda to USD(AT&L) (February 25 and May 5, 2013) in preparation for the AMDR Milestone B decision. Both memoranda highlighted severe shortfalls in the operational test plans in the AMDR and DDG 51 Flight III ship self-defense test arena and stressed the requirement for an unmanned SDTS equipped with the AMDR and DDG 51 Flight III Combat System for adequate operational testing of the radar and ship's combat system self-defense capability.

• DOT&E disapproved the AMDR TEMP on May 22, 2013, because the proposed operational test approach did not adequately assess the capability of the AMDR to support the DDG 51 Flight III Destroyer's self-defense mission.

• DOT&E disapproved the Aegis Modernization TEMP on August 9, 2013, because the proposed operational testing did not provide a credible M&S effort needed to fully assess the ship's combat system self-defense capability nor a means to validate the M&S (i.e., an unmanned SDTS equipped with an AMDR and the DDG 51 Flight III Combat System).

Assessment

• The operational test programs for the AMDR, Aegis Modernization, and DDG 51 Flight III Destroyer programs are not adequate to fully assess their self-defense capabilities in addition to being inadequate to test the following Navy-approved AMDR and DDG 51 Flight III requirements.

- The AMDR Capability Development Document describes AMDR's IAMD mission, which requires AMDR to support simultaneous defense against multiple ballistic missile threats and multiple advanced anti-ship cruise missile (ASCM) threats. The Capability Development Document also includes an AMDR minimum track range Key Performance Parameter.

- The DDG 51 Flight III Destroyer has a survivability requirement directly tied to meeting a self-defense requirement threshold against ASCMs described in the Navy's Surface Ship Theater Air and Missile Defense Assessment document of July 2008. It clearly states that area defense will not defeat all the threats, thereby demonstrating that area air defense will not completely attrite all ASCM raids and that individual ships must be capable of defeating ASCM leakers in the self-defense zone.

• Conduct of operational testing with threat‑representative ASCM surrogates in the close-in, self-defense battlespace using manned ships is not possible since current Navy test range safety restrictions preclude testing on manned ships in this region because targets and debris from intercepts will pose an unacceptable risk to personnel at ranges where some of the engagements will take place.

- In addition to stand-off ranges (on the order of 2 to 5 nautical miles for subsonic and supersonic surrogates, respectively), safety restrictions require that supersonic ASCM targets not be flown directly at a manned ship, but at some cross-range offset (approximately 1 nautical mile), which unacceptably degrades the operational realism of the test.

- Similar range safety restrictions will preclude testing the AMDR minimum track range requirement against supersonic, sea-skimming ASCM threat-representative surrogates at the land-based AMDR test site at the Pacific Missile Range Facility.

• Due to the inherent complexity and safety limitations, live testing (without an SDTS) cannot provide sufficient data to assess the self-defense capabilities of the AMDR and the DDG 51 Flight III Destroyer.

- M&S will therefore play a major role in determining those capabilities. However, per public law, M&S cannot be the only contributor to the assessment; realistic operational test results are required.

- M&S can support an operational evaluation, but must be accredited not only with manned test ship testing, but also through end-to-end testing against operationally realistic targets equipped with an ADMR and the DDG 51 Flight III Destroyer Combat System in the close-in, self-defense battlespace.

- The extent to which the Navy can use M&S to assess AMDR and DDG 51 Flight III's self-defense capability depends critically on whether the M&S can be rigorously accredited for operational testing.

- Side-by-side comparison between credible live fire test results and M&S test results form the basis for M&S accreditation. Without an Aegis SDTS, there will not be a way to gather the operationally realistic live fire test data needed for comparison to accredit the M&S.

• The Air Warfare/Ship Self Defense Enterprise M&S accreditation paradigm being used in the test programs for LHA-6, Littoral Combat Ship (LCS), DDG 1000, LPD-17, LSD-41/49, and CVN-78 ship classes was approved by the Navy and DOT&E in 2005. It is based on live fire events conducted on manned ships and an SDTS, as well as M&S events conducted in the same configuration.

- The live firings conducted in the close-in, self-defense battlespace can only be accomplished with an SDTS due to the range safety restrictions on testing with manned ships.

- For the AMDR and DDG 51 Flight III, the paradigm will be the same; whatever end-to-end M&S tool is developed must be accredited for use in operational testing by comparing live fire results in the close-in battlespace to simulated events in the close-in battlespace.

- Those live fire events can only be conducted on an SDTS equipped with the AMDR and the DDG 51 Flight III Destroyer Combat System. DOT&E considers that paradigm to be the credible template for application by the AMDR and DDG 51 Flight III Destroyer operational test programs.

• The Navy currently models the Aegis Weapon System (AWS) with Lockheed Martin's Multi-Target Effectiveness Determined under Simulation by Aegis (MEDUSA) M&S tool.

- MEDUSA encompasses several components of the AWS including the SPY-1 radar, Command and Decision, and Weapon Control System. MEDUSA models AWS performance down to the system specification and the Navy considers it a high-fidelity simulation of AWS.

- However, it is not a tactical code model; so, its fidelity is ultimately limited to how closely the specification corresponds to the Aegis tactical code (i.e., the specification is how the system is supposed to work while the tactical code is how the system actually works). This adds to the need for realistic live fire shots to support validation efforts.

- By comparison, the Air Warfare/Ship Self Defense Enterprise M&S test bed used for assessing USS San Antonio's (LPD-17) self-defense capabilities used re-hosted SSDS Mk 2 tactical code.

• Recent test events highlight the limitations of specification models like MEDUSA. During Aegis Advanced Capability Build 08 testing in 2011, five AWS software errors were found during live fire events and tracking exercises.

- Three software errors contributed to a failed SM-2 engagement, one to a failed ESSM engagement, and one to several failed simulated engagements during tracking exercises.

- Since these problems involved software coding errors, it is unlikely that a specification model like MEDUSA (which assumes no software errors in tactical code) would account for such issues and hence it would overestimate the combat system's capability.

• Since Aegis employs ESSM in the close-in, self-defense battlespace, understanding ESSM's performance is critical to understanding the self-defense capabilities of the DDG 51 Flight III Destroyer.

- Past DOT&E Annual Reports have stated that the ESSM's operational effectiveness has not been determined. The Navy has not taken action to adequately test the ESSM's operational effectiveness.

- Specifically, because safety limitations preclude ESSM firing in the close-in self-defense battlespace, there are very little test data available concerning ESSM's performance, as installed on Aegis ships, against supersonic ASCM surrogates.

- Any data available regarding ESSM's performance against supersonic ASCM surrogates are from an SSDS- based combat system configuration, using a completely different guidance mode or one that is supported by a different radar suite.

• The cost of building and operating an Aegis SDTS is small when compared to the total cost of the AMDR development/ procurement and the eventual cost of the 22 (plus) DDG 51 Flight III ships that are planned for acquisition ($55+ Billion). Even smaller is the cost of the SDTS compared to the cost of the ships that the DDG 51 Flight III Destroyer is expected to protect (~$450 Billion in new ship construction over the next 30 years).

- If DDG 51 Flight III Destroyers are unable to defend themselves, these other ships are placed at greater risk.

- Moreover, the SDTS is not a one-time investment for only the AMDR/DDG 51 Flight III IOT&E, as it would be available for other testing that cannot be conducted with manned ships (e.g., the ESSM Block 2) and as the combat system capabilities are improved.

Recommendations

• Status of Previous Recommendations. There are no previous recommendations.

• FY13 Recommendations. The Navy should:

1. Program and fund an SDTS equipped with the AMDR and DDG 51 Flight III Combat System in time for the AMDR/DDG 51 Flight III Destroyer IOT&E.

2. Modify the AMDR, Aegis Modernization, and DDG 51 Flight III TEMPs to include a phase of IOT&E using an SDTS equipped with the AMDR and DDG 51 Flight III Combat System.

3. Modify the AMDR, Aegis Modernization, and DDG 51 Flight III TEMPs to include a credible M&S effort that will enable a full assessment of the AMDR and DDG 51 Flight III Combat System's self-defense capabilities.[32]

Lack of Roadmap for Accomplishing Three Things in Cruiser-Destroyer Force

Another issue for Congress concerns the lack of an announced Navy roadmap for accomplishing three things in the cruiser-destroyer force:

- restoring ship growth margins;

- introducing large numbers of ships with integrated electric drive systems or other technologies that could provide ample electrical power for supporting future electrically powered weapons (such as high-power solid state lasers); and

- introducing technologies (such as those for substantially reducing ship crew size) for substantially reducing ship operating and support (O&S) costs. (The potential

---

[32] Department of Defense, *Director, Operational Test and Evaluation, FY 2013 Annual Report*, January 2014, pp. 161-164.

importance of high-power solid state lasers is discussed in the previous section on the Flight III DDG-51's growth margin.)

The Navy's pre-2008 plan to procure DDG-1000 destroyers and then CG(X) cruisers based on the DDG-1000 hull design represented the Navy's roadmap at the time for restoring growth margins, and for introducing into the cruiser-destroyer force significant numbers of ships with integrated electric drive systems and technologies for substantially reducing ship crew sizes. The ending of the DDG-1000 and CG(X) programs in favor of continued procurement of DDG-51s leaves the Navy without an announced roadmap to do these things, because the Flight III DDG-51 will not feature a fully restored growth margin, will not be equipped with an integrated electric drive system or other technologies that could provide ample electrical power for supporting future electrically powered weapons, and will not incorporate features for substantially reducing ship crew size or for otherwise reducing ship O&S costs substantially below that of Flight IIA DDG-51s.

Options for Congress

In general, options for Congress concerning destroyer acquisition include the following:

- approving, rejecting, or modifying the Navy's procurement, advance procurement, and research and development funding requests for destroyers and their associated systems (such as the AMDR);

- establishing conditions for the obligation and expenditure of funding for destroyers and their associated systems; and

- holding hearings, directing reports, and otherwise requesting information from DOD on destroyers and their associated systems.

In addition to these general options, below are some additional acquisition options relating to destroyers that Congress may wish to consider.

Adjunct Radar Ship

The Navy canceled the CG(X) cruiser program in favor of developing and procuring Flight III DDG-51s reportedly in part on the grounds that the Flight III destroyer would use data from off-board sensors to augment data collected by its AMDR.[33] If those off-board sensors turn out to be less capable than the Navy assumed when it decided to cancel the CG(X) in favor of the Flight III DDG-51, the Navy may need to seek other means for augmenting the data collected by the Flight III DDG-51's AMDR.

One option for doing this would be to procure an adjunct radar ship—a non-combat ship equipped with a large radar that would be considerably more powerful than the Flight III DDG-51's AMDR. The presence in the fleet of a ship equipped with such a radar could significantly improve the fleet's AAW and BMD capabilities. The ship might be broadly similar to (but perhaps less complex and less expensive than) the new Cobra Judy Replacement missile range

---

[33] Amy Butler, "STSS Prompts Shift in CG(X) Plans," *Aerospace Daily & Defense Report*, December 11, 2009: 1-2.

instrumentation ship (**Figure 3**),[34] which is equipped with two large and powerful radars, and which has an estimated total acquisition cost of about $1.7 billion.[35] One to a few such adjunct radar ships might be procured, depending on the number of theaters to be covered, requirements for maintaining forward deployments of such ships, and their homeporting arrangements. The ships would have little or no self-defense capability and would need to be protected in threat situations by other Navy ships.

---

[34] As described by DOD,

> The COBRA JUDY REPLACEMENT (CJR) program replaces the capability of the current United States Naval Ship (USNS) Observation Island (OBIS), its COBRA JUDY radar suite, and other mission essential systems. CJR will fulfill the same mission as the current COBRA JUDY/OBIS. CJR will collect foreign ballistic missile data in support of international treaty verification.
>
> CJR represents an integrated mission solution: ship, radar suite, and other Mission Equipment (ME). CJR will consist of a radar suite including active S-Band and X-Band Phased Array Radars (PARs), weather equipment, and a Mission Communications Suite (MCS). The radar suite will be capable of autonomous volume search and acquisition. The S-Band PAR will serve as the primary search and acquisition sensor and will be capable of tracking and collecting data on a large number of objects in a multi-target complex. The X-Band PAR will provide very high-resolution data on particular objects of interest....
>
> The OBIS replacement platform, USNS Howard O. Lorenzen (Missile Range Instrumentation Ship (T-AGM) 25), is a commercially designed and constructed ship, classed to American Bureau of Shipping standards, certified by the U.S. Coast Guard in accordance with Safety of Life at Sea, and in compliance with other commercial regulatory body rules and regulations, and other Military Sealift Command (MSC) standards. The ship will be U.S. flagged, operated by a Merchant Marine or MSC Civilian Mariner crew, with a minimum of military specifications. The ship is projected to have a 30-year operating system life-cycle.
>
> The U.S. Navy will procure one CJR for the U.S. Air Force using only Research, Development, Test and Evaluation funding. CJR will be turned over to the U.S. Air Force at Initial Operational Capability for all operations and maintenance support....
>
> Program activities are currently focused on installation and final integration of the X and S-band radars onto the ship at Kiewit Offshore Services (KOS) following completion of radar production and initial Integration and Test (I&T) at Raytheon and Northrop Grumman (NG). Raytheon and its subcontractors have completed I&T of the X-band radar and X/S ancillary equipment at KOS. The S-band radar arrived at KOS on February 19, 2011. The United States Naval Ship (USNS) Howard O. Lorenzen (Missile Range Instrumentation Ship (T-AGM) 25) completed at-sea Builder's Trials (BT) in March 2011. The ship is expected to depart VT Halter Marine (VTHM) and arrive at KOS in the third quarter of Fiscal Year 2011 (3QFY11).
>
> (Department of Defense, *Selected Acquisition Report (SAR), Cobra Judy Replacement*, December 31, 2010, pp. 3-5.)

[35] Department of Defense, *Selected Acquisition Report (SAR), Cobra Judy Replacement*, December 31, 2010, p. 13.

Figure 3. Cobra Judy Replacement Ship

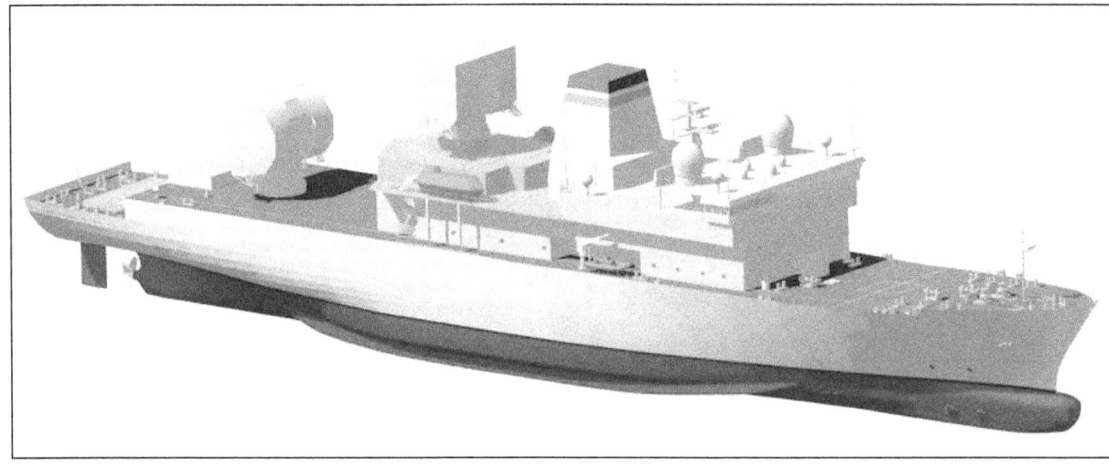

Source: Naval Research Laboratory (http://www.nrl.navy.mil/PressReleases/2010/image1_74-10r_hires.jpg, accessed on April 19, 2011).

Flight III DDG-51 With Increased Capabilities

Another option would be to design the Flight III DDG-51 to have greater capabilities than what the Navy is currently envisioning. Doing this might well require the DDG-51 hull to be lengthened—something that the Navy currently does not appear to be envisioning for the Flight III design. Navy and industry studies on the DDG-51 hull design that were performed years ago suggested that the hull has the potential for being lengthened by as much as 55 feet to accommodate additional systems. Building the Flight III DDG-51 to a lengthened configuration could make room for additional power-generation and cooling equipment, additional vertical launch system (VLS) missile tubes, and larger growth margins. It might also permit a redesign of the deckhouse to support a larger and more capable version of the AMDR than the 14-foot diameter version currently planned for the Flight III DDG-51. Building the Flight III DDG-51 to a lengthened configuration would increase its development cost and its unit procurement cost. The increase in unit procurement cost could reduce the number of Flight III DDG-51s that the Navy could afford to procure without reducing funding for other programs.

DDG-1000 Variant With AMDR

Another option would be to design and procure a version of the DDG-1000 destroyer that is equipped with the AMDR and capable of BMD operations. Such a ship might be more capable in some regards than the Flight III DDG-51, but it might also be more expensive to develop and procure. An AMDR-equipped, BMD-capable version of the DDG-1000 could be pursued as either a replacement for the Flight III DDG-51 or a successor to the Flight III DDG-51 (after some number of Flight III DDG-51s were procured). A new estimate of the cost to develop and procure an AMDR-equipped, BMD-capable version of the DDG-1000 might differ from the estimate in the Navy's 2009 destroyer hull/radar study (the study that led to the Navy's decision to stop DDG-1000 procurement and resume DDG-51 procurement) due to the availability of updated cost information for building the current DDG-1000 design.

New-Design Destroyer

Another option would be to design and procure a new-design destroyer that is intermediate in size between the DDG-51 and DDG-1000 designs, equipped with the AMDR, and capable of BMD operations. This option could be pursued as either a replacement for the Flight III DDG-51 or a successor to the Flight III DDG-51 (after some number of Flight III DDG-51s were procured). Such a ship might be designed with the following characteristics:

- either the same version of the AMDR that is envisioned for the Flight III DDG-51, or a version that is larger (but not as large as the one envisioned for the CG[X]);

- enough electrical power and cooling capacity to permit the ship to be backfitted in the future with a high-power SSL;

- more growth margin than on the Flight III DDG-51;

- producibility features for reducing construction cost per ton that are more extensive than those on the DDG-51 design;

- automation features permitting a crew that is smaller than what can be achieved on a Flight III DDG-51, so as to reduce ship O&S costs;

- physical open-architecture features that are more extensive than those on the Flight III DDG-51, so as to reduce modernization-related life-cycle ownership costs;

- no technologies not already on, or being developed for, other Navy ships, with the possible exception of technologies that would enable an integrated electric drive system that is more compact than the one used on the DDG-1000; and

- DDG-51-like characteristics in other areas, such as survivability, maximum speed, cruising range, and weapons payload.

Such a ship might have a full load displacement of roughly 11,000 to 12,000 tons, compared to about 10,000 tons for the Flight III DDG-51, 15,000 or more tons for an AAW/BMD version of the DDG-1000, and perhaps 15,000 to 23,000 tons for a CG(X).[36]

A March 18, 2013, press report states that

---

[36] The cost and technical risk of developing the new destroyer's hull design could be minimized by leveraging, where possible, existing surface combatant hull designs. The cost and technical risk of developing its combat system could be minimized by using a modified version of the DDG-51 or DDG-1000 combat system. Other development costs and risks for the new destroyer would be minimized by using no technologies not already on, or being developed for, other Navy ships (with the possible exception of some integrated electric drive technologies). Even with such steps, however, the cost and technical risk of developing the new destroyer would be greater than those of the Flight III DDG-51. The development cost of the new destroyer would likely be equivalent to the procurement cost of at least one destroyer, and possibly two destroyers.

The procurement cost of the new destroyer would be minimized by incorporating producibility features for reducing construction cost per ton that are more extensive than those on the Flight III DDG-51. Even with such features, the new destroyer would be more expensive to procure than the Flight III DDG-51, in part because the Flight III DDG-51 would leverage many years of prior production of DDG-51s. In addition, the new destroyer, as a new ship design, would pose more risk of procurement cost growth than would the Flight III DDG-51. The procurement cost of the new destroyer would nevertheless be much less than that of the CG(X), and might, after the production of the first few units, be fairly close to that of the Flight III DDG-51.

A recommended reevaluation of the next flights of LCSs [Littoral Combat Ships][37]... is only part of a classified memo, "Vision for the 2025 Surface Fleet," submitted late last year by the head of Naval Surface Forces, Vice Adm. Tom Copeman, to Chief of Naval Operations Adm. Jon Greenert....

Copeman, according to several sources familiar with the document, also recommended against building the DDG 51 Flight III destroyers, a modification of the Arleigh Burke class to be fitted with the new Air Missile Defense Radar (AMDR) under development to replace the SPY-1 radars used in Aegis warships. The AMDR, designed with higher power and fidelity to handle the complex ballistic-missile defense mission, will require significantly more electrical power than the current system. And, while the AMDR apparently will fit into the DDG 51 hull, margins for future growth are severely limited.

Instead, sources said Copeman recommends creating a new, large surface combatant fitted with AMDR and designed with the power, weight and space to field "top-end energy weapons" like the electromagnetic rail gun under development by the Navy.

The new ship could also be developed into a replacement for today's Ticonderoga-class missile cruisers in the air defense mission of protecting deployed aircraft carriers—a mission Copeman says needs to be preserved. All flattops have a "shotgun" cruiser that accompanies them throughout a deployment, but the missile ships are aging and, by 2025, only four will remain in service to protect the fleet's 11 carriers.

The Navy prefers cruisers over destroyers for the role because of the bigger ships' extra missile fire control channels, their more senior commanders and a better ability to tow the carrier should it be disabled.

While recommending against the Flight III, Copeman would continue building the existing DDG 51 Flight IIA variant until a new design is available.[38]

Legislative Activity for FY2014

FY2014 Funding Request

The Navy's proposed FY2014 budget requested $1,615.6 million to complete the procurement funding for the one DDG-51 requested for procurement in FY2014. The Navy estimated the total procurement cost of this ship at $1,729.7 million, and the ship has received $114.1 million in prior-year advance procurement (AP) funding. The FY2014 budget also requested $388.6 million in AP funding for DDG-51s to be procured in future fiscal years. The Navy's proposed FY2014 budget also requested $231.7 million in procurement funding to help complete procurement costs for three Zumwalt (DDG-1000) class destroyers procured in FY2007-FY2009, and $240.1 million in research and development funding for the AMDR. The funding request for the AMDR is contained in the Navy's research and development account in Project 3186 ("Air and Missile Defense Radar") of Program Element (PE) 0604501N ("Advanced Above Water Sensors").

---

[37] For more on the LCS program, see CRS Report RL33741, *Navy Littoral Combat Ship (LCS) Program: Background and Issues for Congress*, by Ronald O'Rourke.

[38] Christopher P. Cavas, "U.S. Navy Weighs Halving LCS Order," *Defense News*, March 18, 2013: 1.

FY2014 National Defense Authorization Act (H.R. 3304/P.L. 113-66)

House (Committee Report)

The House Armed Services Committee, in its report (H.Rept. 113-102 of June 7, 2013) on the FY2014 National Defense Authorization Act (H.R. 1960), recommends increasing by $332 million the Navy's request for FY2014 procurement funding for the DDG-51 program, approving the Navy's request for FY2014 advance procurement (AP) funding for the DDG-51 program, and increasing by $79.3 million the Navy's request for FY2014 procurement funding for the DDG-1000 program. (Page 387, lines 007, 008, 009, and 020.)

The $332 million in additional procurement funding recommended for the DDG-51 program is approximately what the Navy has testified would be needed to restore full funding for the third DDG-51 procured in FY2013 (i.e., the 10th DDG-51 in the FY2013-FY2017 MYP contract for the DDG-51 program) following the March 1, 2013, sequester. The $79.3 million in additional procurement funding recommended for the DDG-1000 program is $9 million more than the $70.3 million that was sequestered from the program in the March 1, 2013, sequester.

H.Rept. 113-102 also recommends approving the Navy's request for FY2014 research and development funding for PE 0604501N ("Advanced Above Water Sensors"), which includes $240.1 million in requested funding for the AMDR (page 431, line 107). Regarding the AMDR, the report states:

> *Air and Missile Defense Radar deployment on naval vessels*
>
> The Navy has reported that the Air and Missile Defense Radar (AMDR) suite is being developed to fulfill Integrated Air and Missile Defense requirements for multiple ship classes. This suite consists of an S-band radar (AMDR-S), an X-band radar and a Radar Suite Controller. AMDR would provide multi-mission capabilities, simultaneously supporting long-range, exoatmospheric detection, tracking and discrimination of ballistic missiles, as well as Area and Self Defense against air and surface threats. For the ballistic missile defense capability, increased radar sensitivity and bandwidth over current radar systems are needed to detect, track, and support engagements of advanced ballistic missile threats at the required ranges, concurrent with Area and Self Defense against Air and Surface threats. For the Area Air Defense and Self Defense capability, increased sensitivity and clutter capability is needed to detect, react to, and engage stressing Very Low Observable/Very Low Flyer threats in the presence of heavy land, sea, and rain clutter.
>
> According to the Government Accountability Office report "Assessments of Selected Weapons Programs" (GAO–13–294SP) from March 2013, "the Navy plans to install a 14-foot variant of AMDR on Flight III DDG 51s starting in 2019. According to draft AMDR documents, a 14-foot radar is needed to meet threshold requirements, but an over 20-foot radar is required to fully meet the Navy's desired integrated air and missile defense needs."
>
> The committee supports the continued development of the AMDR capability, but is concerned about the physical limitations associated with the future deployment of this capability on the Arleigh Burke-class Destroyer Flight III. Therefore, the committee directs the Secretary of the Navy to submit a report to the congressional defense committees by March 1, 2014, that addresses the following:
>
> (1) The capability requirements associated with the AMDR;

(2) Required space, cooling and electrical distribution upgrades necessary to support AMDR on the Arleigh Burke-class Destroyer Flight III;

(3) An assessment as to whether the limitations associated with the Arleigh Burke-class Destroyer Flight III will negatively impact the deployment on AMDR;

(4) An assessment of the deployment of AMDR on other naval platforms including the San Antonio-class Amphibious Transport Dock; and

(5) An assessment of the expansion capacity of the Arleigh Burke-class Destroyer Flight III to support further spiral development associated with future weapons. (Pages 26-27)

House (Floor Consideration)

On June 13, 2013, as part of its consideration of H.R. 1960, the House agreed to by voice vote H.Amdt. 164, an en bloc amendment that included, among other things, amendment Number 103 from H.Rept. 113-108 of June 13 (legislative day, June 12), 2013, which provided for the further consideration of H.R. 1960. Amendment Number 103 became Section 1026 of H.R. 1960 as passed by the House. The text of Section 1026 is as follows:

> SEC. 1026. REPORT COMPARING COSTS OF DDG 1000 AND DDG 51 FLIGHT III SHIPS.
>
> Not later than March 15, 2014, the Secretary of the Navy shall submit to the congressional defense committees a report providing an updated comparison of the costs and risks of acquiring DDG 1000 and DDG 51 Flight III vessels equipped for enhanced ballistic missile defense capability. The report shall include each of the following:
>
> (1) An updated estimate of the total cost to develop, procure, operate, and support ballistic missile defense capable DDG 1000 destroyers equipped with the air and missile defense radar that would be procured in addition to the three prior-year-funded DDG 1000 class ships, and in lieu of Flight III DDG-51 destroyers.
>
> (2) The estimate of the Secretary of the total cost of the current plan to develop, procure, operate, and support Flight III DDG 51 destroyers.
>
> (3) Details on the assumed ballistic missile defense requirements and construction schedules for both the DDG 1000 and DDG 51 Flight III destroyers referred to in paragraphs (1) and (2), respectively.
>
> (4) An updated comparison of the program risks and the resulting ship capabilities in all dimensions (not just ballistic missile defense) of the options referred to in paragraphs (1) and (2).
>
> (5) Any other information the Secretary determines appropriate.

Senate

The Senate Armed Services Committee, in its report (S.Rept. 113-44 of June 20, 2013) on S. 1197, recommends increasing by $100 million the Navy's request for FY2014 procurement funding for the DDG-51 program, approving the Navy's request for FY2014 advance procurement (AP) funding for the DDG-51 program, and approving the Navy's request for

FY2014 procurement funding for the DDG-1000 program. The $100 million in additional procurement funding recommended for the DDG-51 program is to "Help buy [a] 3rd DDG–51 in FY[20]13." (Page 296, lines 7, 8, 9, and 20.) S.Rept. 113-44 states:

> Congress added $1.0 billion to the fiscal year 2013 budget request to purchase an additional DDG–51 beyond the two DDG–51s in the budget request. After the implementation of sequestration earlier this year, the Navy found that sequestration left the Navy several hundred million dollars short of having enough funds to award the contract for the third ship.
>
> The committee specifically recommended multiyear procurement authority last year that allowed for buying this extra ship and believes that the Navy should buy the extra ship to help meet force structure shortfalls.
>
> The committee recommends an increase of $100.0 million in SCN for completion of prior year shipbuilding programs to help buy this additional DDG–51. (Page 18)

S.Rept. 113-44 also recommends approving the Navy's request for FY2014 research and development funding for PE 0604501N ("Advanced Above Water Sensors"), which includes $240.1 million in requested funding for the AMDR (page 339, line 107).

Section 123 of H.R. 1960 as reported states:

> SEC. 123. REPEAL OF REQUIREMENTS RELATING TO PROCUREMENT OF FUTURE SURFACE COMBATANTS.
>
> Section 125 of the National Defense Authorization Act for Fiscal Year 2010 (P.L. 111-84; 123 Stat. 2214; 10 U.S.C. 7291 note) is repealed.

Regarding Section 123, S.Rept. 113-44 states:

> **Repeal of requirements relating to procurement of future surface combatants (sec. 123)**
>
> The committee recommends a provision that would repeal section 125 of the National Defense Authorization Act for Fiscal Year 2010 (Public Law 111–84). Under section 125, the Navy was prohibited from obligating or expending funds for construction of, or advance procurement of materials for, naval surface combatants to be constructed after fiscal year 2011 until the Secretary of the Navy had provided specific reports to Congress. The report submitted by the Secretary of the Navy to Congress of February 2010 provided the Department of the Navy's implementation plan to complete these reports. (Page 11)

Final version

The final version of the FY2014 National Defense Authorization Act (H.R. 3304/P.L. 113-66 of December 26, 2013)), recommends increasing by $100 million the Navy's request for FY2014 procurement funding for the DDG-51 program, so as to "Help buy [a] 3rd DDG–51 in FY[20]13," approving the Navy's request for FY2014 advance procurement (AP) funding for the DDG-51 program, and approving the Navy's request for FY2014 procurement funding for the DDG-1000 program (see lines 007, 008, 009, and 020 on pdf page 402 of 532 of the explanatory statement for H.R. 3304).

The act recommends reducing by $79.8 million the Navy's request for FY2014 research and development funding for PE 0604501N ("Advanced Above Water Sensors"), which includes

$240.1 million in requested funding for the AMDR, with the reduction being for "Air and missile defense radar contract delay" (see line 107 on pdf page 440 of 532 of the explanatory statement for H.R. 3304).

Section 122 of the act repealed Section 125 of the FY2010 National Defense Authorization Act (H.R. 2647/P.L. 111-84 of October 28, 2009).[39]

---

[39] The text of Section 125 of H.R. 2647/P.L. 111-84 is as follows:

SEC. 125. PROCUREMENT PROGRAMS FOR FUTURE NAVAL SURFACE COMBATANTS.

(a) Limitation on Availability of Funds Pending Reports About Surface Combatant Shipbuilding Programs- The Secretary of the Navy may not obligate or expend funds for the construction of, or advanced procurement of materials for, a surface combatant to be constructed after fiscal year 2011 until the Secretary has submitted to Congress each of the following:

(1) An acquisition strategy for such surface combatants that has been approved by the Under Secretary of Defense for Acquisition, Technology, and Logistics.

(2) Certification that the Joint Requirements Oversight Council--

(A) has been briefed on the acquisition strategy to procure such surface combatants; and

(B) has concurred that such strategy is the best preferred approach to deliver required capabilities to address future threats, as reflected in the latest assessment by the defense intelligence community.

(3) A verification by, and conclusions of, an independent review panel that, in evaluating the program or programs concerned, the Secretary of the Navy considered each of the following:

(A) Modeling and simulation, including war gaming conclusions regarding combat effectiveness for the selected ship platforms as compared to other reasonable alternative approaches.

(B) Assessments of platform operational availability.

(C) Life cycle costs, including vessel manning levels, to accomplish missions.

(D) The differences in cost and schedule arising from the need to accommodate new sensors and weapons in surface combatants to be constructed after fiscal year 2011 to counter the future threats referred to in paragraph (2), when compared with the cost and schedule arising from the need to accommodate sensors and weapons on surface combatants as contemplated by the 2009 shipbuilding plan for the vessels concerned.

(4) The conclusions of a joint review by the Secretary of the Navy and the Director of the Missile Defense Agency setting forth additional requirements for investment in Aegis ballistic missile defense beyond the number of DDG-51 and CG-47 vessels planned to be equipped for this mission area in the budget of the President for fiscal year 2010 (as submitted to Congress pursuant to section 1105 of title 31, United States Code).

(b) Future Surface Combatant Acquisition Strategy- Not later than the date upon which the President submits to Congress the budget for fiscal year 2012 (as so submitted), the Secretary of the Navy shall submit to the congressional defense committees an update to the open architecture report to Congress that reflects the Navy's combat systems acquisition plans for the surface combatants to be procured in fiscal year 2012 and fiscal years thereafter.

(c) Naval Surface Fire Support- Not later than 120 days after the enactment of this Act, the Secretary of the Navy shall submit to the congressional defense committees an update to the March 2006 Report to Congress on Naval Surface Fire Support. The update shall identify how the Department of Defense intends to address any shortfalls between required naval surface fire support capability and the plan of the Navy to provide that capability. The update shall include addenda by the Chief of Naval Operations and Commandant of the Marine Corps, as was the case in the 2006 report.

(d) Technology Roadmap for Future Surface Combatants and Fleet Modernization-

(1) IN GENERAL- Not later than 120 days after the date of the enactment of this Act, the Secretary of the Navy shall develop a plan to incorporate into surface combatants constructed after 2011, and into fleet modernization programs, the technologies developed for the DDG-1000 destroyer and the DDG-51 and CG-47 Aegis ships, including technologies and systems designed to achieve significant manpower savings.

(continued...)

Section 1027 of the act states:

SEC. 1027. MODIFICATION OF POLICY RELATING TO MAJOR COMBATANT VESSELS OF THE STRIKE FORCES OF THE NAVY.

Section 1012 of the National Defense Authorization Act for Fiscal Year 2008 (10 U.S.C. 7291 note) is amended--

(1) by striking subsection (a) and redesignating subsections (b) and (c) as subsections (a) and (b), respectively; and

(2) in subsection (a), as so redesignated--

(A) by striking `the request shall be for' and inserting `the request shall include a specific assessment of'; and

(B) by inserting `in the analysis of alternatives' after `nuclear power system'.[40]

(...continued)

(2) SCOPE OF PLAN- The plan required by paragraph (1) shall include sufficient detail for systems and subsystems to ensure that the plan--

(A) avoids redundant development for common functions;

(B) reflects implementation of Navy plans for achieving an open architecture for all naval surface combat systems; and

(C) fosters competition.

(e) Definitions- In this section:

(1) The term `2009 shipbuilding plan' means the 30-year shipbuilding plan submitted to Congress pursuant to section 231, title 10, United States Code, together with the budget of the President for fiscal year 2009 (as submitted to Congress pursuant to section 1105 of title 31, United States Code).

(2) The term `surface combatant' means a cruiser, a destroyer, or any naval vessel, excluding Littoral Combat Ships, under a program currently designated as a future surface combatant program.

[40] The text of Section 1012 of the FY2008 National Defense Authorization Act (H.R. 4986/P.L. 110-181 of January 28, 2008) is as follows:

SEC. 1012. POLICY RELATING TO MAJOR COMBATANT VESSELS OF THE STRIKE FORCES OF THE UNITED STATES NAVY.

(a) Integrated Nuclear Power Systems- It is the policy of the United States to construct the major combatant vessels of the strike forces of the United States Navy, including all new classes of such vessels, with integrated nuclear power systems.

(b) Requirement To Request Nuclear Vessels- If a request is submitted to Congress in the budget for a fiscal year for construction of a new class of major combatant vessel for the strike forces of the United States, the request shall be for such a vessel with an integrated nuclear power system, unless the Secretary of Defense submits with the request a notification to Congress that the inclusion of an integrated nuclear power system in such vessel is not in the national interest.

(c) Definitions- In this section:

(1) MAJOR COMBATANT VESSELS OF THE STRIKE FORCES OF THE UNITED STATES NAVY- The term `major combatant vessels of the strike forces of the United States Navy' means the following:

(A) Submarines.

(B) Aircraft carriers.

(C) Cruisers, battleships, or other large surface combatants whose primary mission includes protection of carrier strike groups, expeditionary strike groups, and vessels comprising a sea base.

(continued...)

Regarding Section 1027, the explanatory statement for H.R. 3304 states:

Modification of policy relating to major combatant vessels of the strike forces of the Navy (sec. 1027)

The Senate committee-reported bill contained a provision (sec. 1023) that would repeal section 1012 of the National Defense Authorization Act for Fiscal Year 2008 (P.L. 110-181). That section requires that the Navy build any new class of major surface combatant and amphibious assault ship with an integrated nuclear power system, unless the Secretary of the Navy notifies the congressional defense committees that, as a result of a cost-benefit analysis, it would not be practical for the Navy to design the class of ships with an integrated nuclear power system.

The House bill contained no similar provision.

The agreement includes the Senate provision with an amendment that would amend section 1021 to: (1) delete the requirement to include integrated nuclear power systems in any new ship class, and (2) add the requirement that the Navy analyze integrated nuclear power alternative in its analysis of alternatives for new ship classes, and report the results of that analysis in the budget request. (pdf page 203 of 532)

Section 1025 of the act states:

SEC. 1025. REPORT COMPARING COSTS OF DDG 1000 AND DDG 51 FLIGHT III SHIPS.

Not later than March 15, 2014, the Secretary of the Navy shall submit to the congressional defense committees a report providing an updated comparison of the costs and risks of acquiring DDG 1000 and DDG 51 Flight III vessels equipped for enhanced ballistic missile defense capability. The report shall include each of the following:

(1) An updated estimate of the total cost to develop, procure, operate, and support ballistic missile defense capable DDG 1000 destroyers equipped with the air and missile defense radar.

(2) The estimate of the Secretary of the total cost of the current plan to develop, procure, operate, and support Flight III DDG 51 destroyers.

(3) Details on the assumed ballistic missile defense requirements and construction schedules for both the DDG 1000 and DDG 51 Flight III destroyers referred to in paragraphs (1) and (2), respectively.

(4) An updated comparison of the program risks and the resulting ship capabilities in all dimensions (not just ballistic missile defense) of the options referred to in paragraphs (1) and (2).

(...continued)

(2) INTEGRATED NUCLEAR POWER SYSTEM- The term `integrated nuclear power system' means a ship engineering system that uses a naval nuclear reactor as its energy source and generates sufficient electric energy to provide power to the ship's electrical loads, including its combat systems and propulsion motors.

(3) BUDGET- The term `budget' means the budget that is submitted to Congress by the President under section 1105(a) of title 31, United States Code.

(5) Any other information the Secretary determines appropriate.

FY2014 DOD Appropriations Act (Division C of H.R. 3547/P.L. 113-76)

House

The House Appropriations Committee, in its report (H.Rept. 113-113 of June 17, 2013) on the FY2014 DOD Appropriations Act (H.R. 2397), recommends approving the Navy's request for FY2014 procurement funding for the DDG-51 program, approving the Navy's request for FY2014 advance procurement (AP) funding for the DDG-51 program, and approving the Navy's request for FY2014 procurement funding for the DDG-1000 program. (Page 163, lines 7, 8, and 9.)

H.Rept. 113-113 recommends reducing by $82.8 million the Navy's request for FY2014 research and development funding for PE 0604501N ("Advanced Above Water Sensors"), which includes $240.1 million in requested funding for the AMDR. (Page 226, line 107). Of the recommended reduction of $82.8 million, $79.8 million is for "Air and missile defense radar contract delay." (Page 234, line 107.)

Senate

The Senate Appropriations Committee, in its report (S.Rept. 113-85 of August 1, 2013) on the FY2014 DOD Appropriations Act (S. 1429), recommends increasing by $100 million the Navy's request for FY2014 procurement funding for the DDG-51 program, with the increase being for "Authorization adjustment: DDG–51," reducing by $9 million the Navy's request for FY2014 advance procurement (AP) funding for the DDG-51 program, with the reduction being for "Restoring acquisition accountability: Flight III Advance Planning early to need," and approving the Navy's request for FY2014 procurement funding for the DDG-1000 program. (Page 100, lines 7, 8, 9, and 20, and page 101, lines 9 and 20). The $100 million in additional DDG-51 procurement funding is provided in the line item for completion of prior-year shipbuilding (line 20), and is noted in **Section 8072** of S. 1429 as reported by the committee, which concerns funding for this line item. S.Rept. 113-85 states:

> *DDG–51 Destroyer.*—The Committee understands that the DDG–51 program has a $304,000,000 shortfall due to prior year sequestration reductions, and recommends an additional $100,000,000 for the DDG–51 to allow the Navy to award the tenth DDG–51 under the current multi-year procurement contract, as previously authorized and appropriated. The Committee understands that its fiscal year 2014 shipbuilding recommendations create an outyear asset for the Navy to apply to shortfalls. (Page 102)

S.Rept. 113-85 recommends reducing by $87 million the Navy's request for FY2014 research and development funding for PE 0604501N ("Advanced Above Water Sensors"), which includes $240.1 million in requested funding for the AMDR, with the reduction being for "Restoring acquisition accountability: AMDR MS [Milestone] B 8 month schedule delay." (Page 156, line 107, and page 159, line 107.) S.Rept. 113-85 states:

> *Air and Missile Defense Radar.*—The fiscal year 2014 request includes $275,871,000 to continue the engineering and manufacturing development phase. The Navy originally

planned to award the contract and down select to a single manufacturer in November 2012 which was subsequently delayed to July 2013. As a result of the delay, a majority of the fiscal year 2013 funding will be awarded later than planned. Therefore, the Committee recommends a reduction of $87,000,000. (Page 161)

Final Version

The final version of the FY2014 DOD Appropriations Act (Division C of H.R. 3547/P.L. 113-76 of January 17, 2014) increases by $100 million the Navy's request for FY2014 procurement funding for the DDG-51 program. The additional $100 million is provided in the line that funds the completion of ships procured in prior years, where it is described as being for "DDG-51 authorization adjustment." The act reduces by $19 million the Navy's request for FY2014 advance procurement (AP) funding for the DDG-51 program, with the reduction being for "Flight Ill advance planning ahead of need," and approves the Navy's request for FY2014 procurement funding for the DDG-1000 program (see lines 7, 8, 9, and 20 on pdf pages 159 and 160 of 351 of the explanatory statement for Division C of H.R. 3304). The additional $100 million in DDG-51 procurement funding is also noted in **Section 8072** of the act.

Navy officials have indicated that the additional $100 million in DDG-51 procurement funding provided by the act is enough to permit the Navy to award the third DDG-51 that was procured in FY2013 (i.e.,, the 10th DDG-51 included in the FY2013-FY2017 DDG-51 MYP contract), though an additional $200 million will eventually be needed to complete the ship's funding.[41]

The act reduces by $118 million the Navy's request for FY2014 research and development funding for PE 0604501N ("Advanced Above Water Sensors"), which includes $240.1 million in requested funding for the AMDR, with $115 million of the reduction being for "Air and missile defense radar contract delay" (see line 107 on pdf page 235 of 351 of the explanatory statement for Division C of H.R. 3547.)

---

[41] See, for example, Olga Belogolova, "Omnibus Spending Bill Clears The Way For 10th DDG-51 Destroyer," *Inside the Navy*, January 20, 2013.

Appendix A. Additional Background Information on DDG-1000 Program

This appendix presents additional background information on the DDG-1000 program.

Program Origin

The program known today as the DDG-1000 program was announced on November 1, 2001, when the Navy stated that it was replacing a destroyer-development effort called the DD-21 program, which the Navy had initiated in the mid-1990s, with a new Future Surface Combatant Program aimed at developing and acquiring a family of three new classes of surface combatants:[42]

- **a destroyer called DD(X)** for the precision long-range strike and naval gunfire mission;

- **a cruiser called CG(X)** for the air defense and ballistic missile mission; and

- **a smaller combatant called the Littoral Combat Ship (LCS)** to counter submarines, small surface attack craft (also called "swarm boats"), and mines in heavily contested littoral (near-shore) areas.[43]

On April 7, 2006, the Navy announced that it had redesignated the DD(X) program as the DDG-1000 program. The Navy also confirmed in that announcement that the first ship in the class, DDG-1000, is to be named the *Zumwalt*, in honor of Admiral Elmo R. Zumwalt, the Chief of Naval operations from 1970 to 1974. The decision to name the first ship after Zumwalt was made by the Clinton Administration in July 2000, when the program was still called the DD-21 program.[44]

New Technologies

The DDG-1000 incorporates a significant number of new technologies, including a wave-piercing, tumblehome hull design for reduced detectability,[45] a superstructure made partly of large sections of composite (i.e., fiberglass-like) materials rather than steel or aluminum, an integrated

---

[42] The DD-21 program was part of a Navy surface combatant acquisition effort begun in the mid-1990s and called the SC-21 (Surface Combatant for the 21st Century) program. The SC-21 program envisaged a new destroyer called DD-21 and a new cruiser called CG-21. When the Navy announced the Future Surface Combatant Program in 2001, development work on the DD-21 had been underway for several years, while the start of development work on the CG-21 was still years in the future. The current DDG-1000 destroyer CG(X) cruiser programs can be viewed as the descendants, respectively, of the DD-21 and CG-21. The acronym SC-21 is still used in the Navy's research and development account to designate the line item (i.e., program element) that funds development work on both the DDG-1000 and CG(X).

[43] For more on the LCS program, see CRS Report RL33741, *Navy Littoral Combat Ship (LCS) Program: Background and Issues for Congress*, by Ronald O'Rourke.

[44] For more on Navy ship names, see CRS Report RS22478, *Navy Ship Names: Background for Congress*, by Ronald O'Rourke.

[45] A tumblehome hull slopes inward, toward the ship's centerline, as it rises up from the waterline, in contrast to a conventional flared hull, which slopes outward as it rises up from the waterline.

---

electric-drive propulsion system,[46] a total-ship computing system for moving information about the ship, automation technologies enabling its reduced-sized crew, a dual-band radar, a new kind of vertical launch system (VLS) for storing and firing missiles, and two copies of a 155mm gun called the Advanced Gun System (AGS). The AGS is to fire a new rocket-assisted 155mm shell, called the Long Range Land Attack Projectile (LRLAP), to ranges of more than 60 nautical miles. The DDG-1000 can carry 600 LRLAP rounds (300 for each gun), and additional rounds can be brought aboard the ship while the guns are firing, creating what Navy officials call an "infinite magazine."

Planned Quantity

When the DD-21 program was initiated, a total of 32 ships was envisaged. In subsequent years, the planned total for the DD(X)/DDG-1000 program was reduced to 16 to 24, then to 7, and finally to 3.

Construction Shipyards

Under a DDG-1000 acquisition strategy approved by the Under Secretary of Defense for Acquisition, Technology, and Logistics (USD AT&L) on February 24, 2004, the first DDG-1000 was to have been built by HII/Ingalls, the second ship was to have been built by GD/BIW, and contracts for building the first six were to have been equally divided between HII/Ingalls[47] and GD/BIW.

In February 2005, Navy officials announced that they would seek approval from USD AT&L to instead hold a one-time, winner-take-all competition between HII/Ingalls and GD/BIW to build all DDG-1000s. On April 20, 2005, the USD AT&L issued a decision memorandum deferring this proposal, stating in part, "at this time, I consider it premature to change the shipbuilder portion of the acquisition strategy which I approved on February 24, 2004."

Several Members of Congress also expressed opposition to Navy's proposal for a winner-take-all competition. Congress included a provision (§1019) in the Emergency Supplemental Appropriations Act for 2005 (H.R. 1268/P.L. 109-13 of May 11, 2005) prohibiting a winner-take-all competition. The provision effectively required the participation of at least one additional shipyard in the program but did not specify the share of the program that is to go to the additional shipyard.

On May 25, 2005, the Navy announced that, in light of Section 1019 of P.L. 109-13, it wanted to shift to a "dual-lead-ship" acquisition strategy, under which two DDG-1000s would be procured in FY2007, with one to be designed and built by HII/Ingalls and the other by GD/BIW.

Section 125 of the FY2006 defense authorization act (H.R. 1815/P.L. 109-163) again prohibited the Navy from using a winner-take-all acquisition strategy for procuring its next-generation destroyer. The provision again effectively requires the participation of at least one additional

---

[46] For more on integrated electric-drive technology, see CRS Report RL30622, *Electric-Drive Propulsion for U.S. Navy Ships: Background and Issues for Congress*, by Ronald O'Rourke.

[47] At the time of the events described in this section, HII was owned by Northrop Grumman and was called Northrop Grumman Shipbuilding (NGSB).

shipyard in the program but does not specify the share of the program that is to go to the additional shipyard.

On November 23, 2005, the USD AT&L granted Milestone B approval for the DDG-1000, permitting the program to enter the System Development and Demonstration (SDD) phase. As part of this decision, the USD AT&L approved the Navy's proposed dual-lead-ship acquisition strategy and a low rate initial production quantity of eight ships (one more than the Navy subsequently planned to procure).

On February 14, 2008, the Navy awarded contract modifications to GD/BIW and HII/Ingalls for the construction of the two lead ships. The awards were modifications to existing contracts that the Navy has with GD/BIW and HII/Ingalls for detailed design and construction of the two lead ships. Under the modified contracts, the line item for the construction of the dual lead ships is treated as a cost plus incentive fee (CPIF) item.

Until July 2007, it was expected that HII/Ingalls would be the final-assembly yard for the first DDG-1000 and that GD/BIW would be the final-assembly yard for the second. On September 25, 2007, the Navy announced that it had decided to build the first DDG-1000 at GD/BIW, and the second at HII/Ingalls.

On January 12, 2009, it was reported that the Navy, HII/Ingalls, and GD/BIW in the fall of 2008 began holding discussions on the idea of having GD/BIW build both the first and second DDG-1000s, in exchange for HII/Ingalls receiving a greater share of the new DDG-51s that would be procured under the Navy's July 2008 proposal to stop DDG-1000 procurement and restart DDG-51 procurement.[48]

On April 8, 2009, it was reported that the Navy had reached an agreement with HII/Ingalls and GD/BIW to shift the second DDG-1000 to GD/BIW, and to have GD/BIW build all three ships. HII/Iingalls will continue to make certain parts of the three ships, notably their composite deckhouses. The agreement to have all three DDG-1000s built at GD/BIW was a condition that Secretary of Defense Robert Gates set forth in an April 6, 2009, news conference on the FY2010 defense budget for his support for continuing with the construction of all three DDG-1000s (rather than proposing the cancellation of the second and third).

Procurement Cost Cap

Section 123 of the FY2006 defense authorization act (H.R. 1815/P.L. 109-163 of January 6, 2006) limited the procurement cost of the fifth DDG-1000 to $2.3 billion, plus adjustments for inflation and other factors. Given the truncation of the DDG-1000 program to three ships, this unit procurement cost cap appears moot.

---

[48] Christopher P. Cavas, "Will Bath Build Second DDG 1000?" *Defense News*, January 12, 2009: 1, 6.

2010 Nunn-McCurdy Breach, Program Restructuring, and Milestone Recertification

On February 1, 2010, the Navy notified Congress that the DDG-1000 program had experienced a critical cost breach under the Nunn-McCurdy provision. The Nunn-McCurdy provision (10 U.S.C. 2433a) requires certain actions to be taken if a major defense acquisition program exceeds (i.e., breaches) certain cost-growth thresholds and is not terminated. Among other things, a program that experiences a cost breach large enough to qualify under the provision as a critical cost breach has its previous acquisition system milestone certification revoked. (In the case of the DDG-1000 program, this was Milestone B.) In addition, for the program to proceed rather than be terminated, DOD must certify certain things, including that the program is essential to national security and that there are no alternatives to the program that will provide acceptable capability to meet the joint military requirement at less cost.[49]

The Navy stated in its February 1, 2010, notification letter that the DDG-1000 program's critical cost breach was a mathematical consequence of the program's truncation to three ships.[50] Since the DDG-1000 program has roughly $9.3 billion in research and development costs, truncating the program to three ships increased to roughly $3.1 billion the average amount of research and development costs that are included in the average acquisition cost (i.e., average research and development cost plus procurement cost) of each DDG-1000. The resulting increase in program acquisition unit cost (PAUC)—one of two measures used under the Nunn-McCurdy provision for measuring cost growth[51]—was enough to cause a Nunn-McCurdy critical cost breach.

In a June 1, 2010, letter (with attachment) to Congress, Ashton Carter, the DOD acquisition executive (i.e., the Under Secretary of Defense for Acquisition, Technology and Logistics), stated that he had restructured the DDG-1000 program and that he was issuing the certifications required under the Nunn-McCurdy provision for the restructured DDG-1000 program to proceed.[52] The letter stated that the restructuring of the DDG-1000 program included the following:

- A change to the DDG-1000's design affecting its primary radar.

- A change in the program's Initial Operational Capability (IOC) from FY2015 to FY2016.

- A revision to the program's testing and evaluation requirements.

Regarding the change to the ship's design affecting its primary radar, the DDG-1000 originally was to have been equipped with a dual-band radar (DBR) consisting of the Raytheon-built X-

---

[49] For more on the Nunn-McCurdy provision, see CRS Report R41293, *The Nunn-McCurdy Act: Background, Analysis, and Issues for Congress*, by Moshe Schwartz.

[50] Source: Letter to congressional offices dated February 1, 2010, from Robert O. Work, Acting Secretary of the Navy, to Representative Ike Skelton, provided to CRS by Navy Office of Legislative Affairs on February 24, 2010.

[51] PAUC is the sum of the program's research and development cost and procurement cost divided by the number of units in the program. The other measure used under the Nunn-McCurdy provision to measure cost growth is average program unit cost (APUC), which is the program's total procurement cost divided by the number of units in the program.

[52] Letter dated June 1, 2010, from Ashton Carter, Under Secretary of Defense (Acquisition, Technology and Logistics) to the Honorable Ike Skelton, with attachment. The letter and attachment were posted on InsideDefense.com (subscription required) on June 2, 2010.

---

band SPY-3 multifunction radar (MFR) and the Lockheed-built S-band SPY-4 Volume Search Radar (VSR). (Raytheon is the prime contractor for the overall DBR.) Both parts of the DBR have been in development for the past several years. An attachment to the June 1, 2010, letter stated that, as a result of the program's restructuring, the ship is now to be equipped with "an upgraded multifunction radar [MFR] and no volume search radar [VSR]." The change eliminates the Lockheed-built S-band SPY-4 VSR from the ship's design. The ship might retain a space and weight reservation that would permit the VSR to be backfitted to the ship at a later point. The Navy states that

> As part of the Nunn-McCurdy certification process, the Volume Search Radar (VSR) hardware was identified as an acceptable opportunity to reduce cost in the program and thus was removed from the current baseline design....
>
> Modifications will be made to the SPY-3 Multi-Function Radar (MFR) with the focus of meeting ship Key Performance Parameters. The MFR modifications will involve software changes to perform a volume search functionality. Shipboard operators will be able to optimize the SPY-3 MFR for either horizon search or volume search. While optimized for volume search, the horizon search capability is limited. Without the VSR, DDG 1000 is still expected to perform local area air defense....
>
> The removal of the VSR will result in an estimated $300 million net total cost savings for the three-ship class. These savings will be used to offset the program cost increase as a result of the truncation of the program to three ships. The estimated cost of the MFR software modification to provide the volume search capability will be significantly less than the estimated procurement costs for the VSR.[53]

Regarding the figure of $300 million net total cost savings in the above passage, the Navy during 2011 determined that eliminating the SPY-4 VSR from the DDG-1000 increased by $54 million the cost to integrate the dual-band radar into the Navy's new Gerald R. Ford (CVN-78) class aircraft carriers.[54] Subtracting this $54 million cost from the above $300 million savings figure would bring the net total cost savings to about $246 million on a Navy-wide basis.

A July 26, 2010, press report quotes Captain James Syring, the DDG-1000 program manager, as stating: "We don't need the S-band radar to meet our requirements [for the DDG-1000]," and "You can meet [the DDG-1000's operational] requirements with [the] X-band [radar] with software modifications."[55]

An attachment to the June 1, 2010, letter stated that the PAUC for the DDG-1000 program had increased 86%, triggering the Nunn-McCurdy critical cost breach, and that the truncation of the program to three ships was responsible for 79 of the 86 percentage points of increase. (The attachment stated that the other seven percentage points of increase are from increases in development costs that are primarily due to increased research and development work content for the program.)

---

[53] Source: Undated Navy information paper on DDG-51 program restructuring provided to CRS and CBO by Navy Office of Legislative Affairs on July 19, 2010.

[54] Source: Undated Navy information paper on CVN-78 cost issues, provided by Navy Office of Legislative Affairs to CRS on March 19, 2012.

[55] Cid Standifer, "Volume Radar Contracted For DDG-1000 Could Be Shifted To CVN-79," *Inside the Navy*, July 26, 2010.

Carter also stated in his June 1, 2010, letter that he had directed that the DDG-1000 program be funded, for the period FY2011-FY2015, to the cost estimate for the program provided by the Cost Assessment and Program Evaluation (CAPE) office (which is a part of the Office of the Secretary of Defense [OSD]), and, for FY2016 and beyond, to the Navy's cost estimate for the program. The program was previously funded to the Navy's cost estimate for all years. Since CAPE's cost estimate for the program is higher than the Navy's cost estimate, funding the program to the CAPE estimate for the period FY2011-FY2015 will increase the cost of the program as it appears in the budget for those years. The letter states that DOD "intends to address the [resulting] FY2011 [funding] shortfall [for the DDG-1000 program] through reprogramming actions."

An attachment to the letter stated that the CAPE in May 2010 estimated the PAUC of the DDG-1000 program (i.e., the sum of the program's research and development costs and procurement costs, divided by the three ships in the program) as $7.4 billion per ship in then-year dollars ($22.1 billion in then-year dollars for all three ships), and the program's average procurement unit cost (APUC), which is the program's total procurement cost divided by the three ships in the program, as $4.3 billion per ship in then-year dollars ($12.8 billion in then-year dollars for all three ships). The attachment stated that these estimates are at a confidence level of about 50%, meaning that the CAPE believes there is a roughly 50% chance that the program can be completed at or under these cost estimates, and a roughly 50% chance that the program will exceed these cost estimates.

An attachment to the letter directed the Navy to "return for a Defense Acquisition Board (DAB) review in the fall 2010 timeframe when the program is ready to seek approval of the new Milestone B and authorization for production of the DDG-1002 [i.e., the third ship in the program]."

On October 8, 2010, DOD reinstated the DDG-1000 program's Milestone B certification and authorized the Navy to continue production of the first and second DDG-1000s and commence production of the third DDG-1000.[56]

Under Secretary of Defense Ashton Carter's June 1, 2010, letter and attachment restructuring the DDG-1000 program and DOD's decision on October 8, 2010, to reinstate the DDG-1000 program's Milestone B certification (see **Appendix A**) raise the following potential oversight questions for Congress:

- Why did DOD decide, as part of its restructuring of the DDG-1000 program, to change the primary radar on the DDG-1000?

- What are the potential risks to the DDG-1000 program of changing its primary radar at this stage in the program (i.e., with the first ship under construction, and preliminary construction activities underway on the second ship)?

- How will the upgraded MFR differ in cost, capabilities, and technical risks from the baseline MFR included in the original DDG-1000 design?

- What is the net impact on the capabilities of the DDG-1000 of the change to the DDG-1000's primary radar (i.e., of removing the VSR and upgrading the MFR)?

---

[56] Christopher J. Castelli, "Pentagon Approves Key Milestone For Multibillion-Dollar Destroyer," *Inside the Navy*, November 22, 2010.

- Given change to the DDG-1000's primary radar and the May 2010 CAPE estimates of the program's program acquisition unit cost (PAUC) and average program unit cost (APUC), is the DDG-1000 program still cost effective?

- What impact on cost, schedule, or technical risk, if any, will the removal of the VSR from the DDG-1000 design have on the Navy's plan to install the dual-band radar (DBR), including the VSR, on the Ford (CVN-78) class aircraft carriers CVN-78 and CVN-79?[57]

March 2013 GAO Report

A March 2013 GAO report assessing selected major DOD weapon acquisition programs stated the following of the DDG-1000 program:

Technology Maturity

Three of the program's 11 critical technologies are mature; the remaining 8 technologies will not be demonstrated in a realistic environment until after ship installation. Program officials stated that the Navy received the lead ship's deckhouse in October 2012 and its integration onto the hull was completed in December 2012. Cost and schedule impacts from Ingalls not completing cabling, piping, and foundations prior to delivery are being assessed. Officials reported successful completion of land-based testing to verify compatibility and interoperability with the integrated power system and engineering control system in March 2012. Raytheon completed software coding and started integration and testing for release 6 of the total ship computing environment, and a follow-on software spiral is now under contract. Releases 1 to 5 are complete and certified. Program officials stated that the gun system's long-range land-attack projectile's motor redesign has been successfully tested under various environmental conditions, and other subcomponents will be evaluated during fiscal year 2013 guided flight tests.

Design and Production Maturity

As of December 2012, the first two ships were 80 percent and 48 percent complete respectively, and third ship fabrication began in April 2012. While there have been few design changes resulting from lead ship construction, the rework rate for the lead ship composite deckhouse was 17 percent.

Other Program Issues

In December 2011, the Under Secretary of Defense for Acquisition, Technology, and Logistics (AT&L) delegated the authority for future acquisition decisions to the Navy. The program attributed this shift to cost oversight and risk reduction, noting that average procurement unit cost has decreased $690 million from the 2010 estimate.

The program relies on products, such as the aft peripheral vertical launching system and deckhouse, being transferred from one prime contractor to another. As the integrator, the Navy is responsible for ensuring on-time delivery of products and bears the costs if schedule delays affect another contractor. In 2010 the Navy introduced a joint inspection process whereby the primes and the Navy validate the level of completeness of products prior to

---

[57] For more on these aircraft carriers, see CRS Report RS20643, *Navy Ford (CVN-78) Class Aircraft Carrier Program: Background and Issues for Congress*, by Ronald O'Rourke.

integration with the hull. Program officials believe that this reduces the risk of integration issues and rework because the program office, the Gulf Coast and Bath Supervisors of Shipbuilding, and contractors have a common understanding of the quality of the delivered product.

The Navy has awarded contracts for all elements for the first two ships. Contracts for the third ship deckhouse, hangar, aft peripheral vertical launching system, and mission systems equipment are not yet finalized. Program officials note the Navy continues to leverage actual cost data from the first two ships and other similar programs to inform contract pricing and is considering cost efficient alternatives. The Navy is assessing alternative deckhouse materials, such as steel, which both shipyards report is a feasible alternative to composite.

As requested, we reviewed whether individual subcontracting reports from the prime contractor for the program were accepted on eSRS. The government uses subcontracting reports on eSRS as one method of monitoring small business participation. As of December 2012, eSRS indicated that one of the subcontracting reports for DDG 1000's six contracts have been accepted.

Program Office Comments

The President's fiscal year 2011 budget submission reduced the quantity of the DDG 1000 program to three ships and caused a Nunn-McCurdy breach. AT&L recertified the restructured program in June 2010 and adjusted initial operating capability to 2016. Since then, the Navy has awarded ship construction contracts and advanced gun systems contracts for all three ships and all required software. All critical technologies have at least been demonstrated in a relevant environment. More than 90 percent of the software has completed design, code, unit test, and integration, and it is aligned to ship activation. AT&L stated in a December 2011 acquisition decision memorandum that the Navy is executing the Nunn-McCurdy certified program while recognizing, addressing, and retiring risks. A July 2011 Office of Performance Assessment and Root Cause Analyses review also found that the Navy has taken steps in managing risks. The program office also provided technical comments, which were incorporated as appropriate.[58]

---

[58] Government Accountability Office, *Defense Acquisitions[:] Assessments of Selected Weapon Programs*, GAO-13-294SP, March 2012, p. 56.

Appendix B. Additional Background Information on CG(X) Cruiser Program

Background Information on CG(X) Program

The CG(X) cruiser program was announced by the Navy on November 1, 2001.[59] The Navy wanted to procure as many as 19 CG(X)s as replacements for its 22 CG-47s, which are projected to reach the end of their 35-year service lives between 2021 and 2029. The CG-47s are multi-mission ships with an emphasis on AAW and (for some CG-47s) BMD, and the Navy similarly wanted the CG(X) to be a multi-mission ship with an emphasis on AAW and BMD. The CG(X) was to carry the Air and Missile Defense Radar (AMDR), a new radar that was to be considerably larger and more powerful than the SPY-1 radar carried on the Navy's Aegis ships. Some press reports suggested that a nuclear-powered version of the CG(X) might have had a full load displacement of more than 20,000 tons and a unit procurement cost of $5 billion or more.[60]

The Navy's FY2009 budget called for procuring the first CG(X) in FY2011. Beginning in late 2008, however, it was reported that the Navy had decided to defer the procurement of the first CG(X) by several years, to about FY2017.[61] Consistent with these press reports, on April 6, 2009,

---

[59] The Navy on that date announced that that it was launching a Future Surface Combatant Program aimed at acquiring a family of next-generation surface combatants. This new family of surface combatants, the Navy stated, would include three new classes of ships:

- a destroyer called the DD(X)—later redesignated DDG-1000—for the precision long-range strike and naval gunfire mission,

- a cruiser called the CG(X) for the AAW and BMD mission, and

- a smaller combatant called the Littoral Combat Ship (LCS) to counter submarines, small surface attack craft, and mines in heavily contested littoral (near-shore) areas.

The Future Surface Combatant Program replaced an earlier Navy surface combatant acquisition effort, begun in the mid-1990s, called the Surface Combatant for the 21st Century (SC-21) program. The SC-21 program encompassed a planned destroyer called DD-21 and a planned cruiser called CG-21. When the Navy announced the Future Surface Combatant Program in 2001, development work on the DD-21 had been underway for several years, but the start of development work on the CG-21 was still years in the future. The DD(X) program, now called the DDG-1000 or Zumwalt-class program, is essentially a restructured continuation of the DD-21 program. The CG(X) might be considered the successor, in planning terms, of the CG-21. After November 1, 2001, the acronym SC-21 continued for a time to be used in the Navy's research and development account to designate a line item (i.e., program element) that funded development work on the DDG-1000 and CG(X).

[60] For a discussion of nuclear power for Navy surface ships other than aircraft carriers, see CRS Report RL33946, *Navy Nuclear-Powered Surface Ships: Background, Issues, and Options for Congress*, by Ronald O'Rourke.

[61] Zachary M. Peterson, "Navy Awards Technology Company $128 Million Contract For CG(X) Work," *Inside the Navy*, October 27, 2008. Another press report (Katherine McIntire Peters, "Navy's Top Officer Sees Lessons in Shipbuilding Program Failures," *GovernmentExecutive.com*, September 24, 2008) quoted Admiral Gary Roughead, the Chief of Naval Operations, as saying: "What we will be able to do is take the technology from the DDG-1000, the capability and capacity that [will be achieved] as we build more DDG-51s, and [bring those] together around 2017 in a replacement ship for our cruisers." (Material in brackets in the press report.) Another press report (Zachary M. Peterson, "Part One of Overdue CG(X) AOA Sent to OSD, Second Part Coming Soon," *Inside the Navy*, September 29, 2008) quoted Vice Admiral Barry McCullough, the Deputy Chief of Naval Operations for Integration of Capabilities and Resources, as saying that the Navy did not budget for a CG(X) hull in its proposal for the Navy's budget under the FY2010-FY2015 Future Years Defense Plan (FYDP) to be submitted to Congress in early 2009.

An earlier report (Christopher P. Cavas, "DDG 1000 Destroyer Program Facing Major Cuts," *DefenseNews.com*, July 14, 2008) stated that the CG(X) would be delayed until FY2015 or later. See also Geoff Fein, "Navy Likely To Change (continued...)

Secretary of Defense Robert Gates announced—as part of a series of recommendations for the then-forthcoming FY2010 defense budget—a recommendation to "delay the CG-X next generation cruiser program to revisit both the requirements and acquisition strategy" for the program.[62] The Navy's proposed FY2010 budget deferred procurement of the first CG(X) beyond FY2015.

Cancellation of CG(X) Program

The Navy's FY2011 budget proposed terminating the CG(X) program as unaffordable. The Navy's desire to cancel the CG(X) and instead procure Flight III DDG-51s apparently took shape during 2009: at a June 16, 2009, hearing before the Seapower Subcommittee of the Senate Armed Services Committee, the Navy testified that it was conducting a study on destroyer procurement options for FY2012 and beyond that was examining design options based on either the DDG-51 or DDG-1000 hull form.[63] A January 2009 memorandum from the Department of Defense acquisition executive had called for such a study.[64] In September and November 2009, it was reported that the Navy's study was examining how future requirements for AAW and BMD operations might be met by a DDG-51 or DDG-1000 hull equipped with a new radar.[65] On December 7, 2009, it was reported that the Navy wanted to cancel its planned CG(X) cruiser and instead procure an improved version of the DDG-51.[66] In addition to being concerned about the projected high cost and immature technologies of the CG(X),[67] the Navy reportedly had concluded that it does not need a surface combatant with a version of the AMDR as large and capable as the one envisaged for the CG(X) to adequately perform projected AAW and BMD missions, because the Navy will be able to augment data collected by surface combatant radars with data collected by space-based sensors. The Navy reportedly concluded that using data collected by other sensors would permit projected AAW and BMD missions to be performed

---

(...continued)

CG(X)'s Procurement Schedule, Official Says," *Defense Daily*, June 24, 2008; Rebekah Gordon, "Navy Agrees CG(X) By FY-11 Won't Happen But Reveals Little Else," *Inside the Navy*, June 30, 2008.

[62] Source: Opening remarks of Secretary of Defense Robert Gates at an April 6, 2009, news conference on DOD recommendations for the then-forthcoming FY2010 defense budget.

[63] Source: Transcript of spoken remarks of Vice Admiral Bernard McCullough at a June 16, 2009, hearing on Navy force structure shipbuilding before the Seapower subcommittee of the Senate Armed Services Committee.

[64] A January 26, 2009, memorandum for the record from John Young, the then-DOD acquisition executive, stated that "The Navy proposed and OSD [the Office of the Secretary of Defense] agreed with modification to truncate the DDG-1000 Program to three ships in the FY 2010 budget submission." The memo proposed procuring one DDG-51 in FY2010 and two more FY2011, followed by the procurement in FY2012-FY2015 (in annual quantities of 1, 2, 1, 2) of a ship called the Future Surface Combatant (FSC) that could be based on either the DDG-51 design or the DDG-1000 design. The memorandum stated that the FSC might be equipped with a new type of radar, but the memorandum did not otherwise specify the FSC's capabilities. The memorandum stated that further analysis would support a decision on whether to base the FSC on the DDG-51 design or the DDG-1000 design. (Memorandum for the record dated January 26, 2009, from John Young, Under Secretary of Defense [Acquisition, Technology and Logistics], entitled "DDG 1000 Program Way Ahead," posted on InsideDefense.com [subscription required].)

[65] Zachary M. Peterson, "Navy Slated To Wrap Up Future Destroyer Hull And Radar Study," *Inside the Navy*, September 7, 2009. Christopher P. Cavas, "Next-Generation U.S. Warship Could Be Taking Shape," *Defense News*, November 2, 2009: 18, 20.

[66] Christopher J. Castelli, "Draft Shipbuilding Report Reveals Navy Is Killing CG(X) Cruiser Program," *Inside the Navy*, December 7, 2009.

[67] Christopher J. Castelli, "Draft Shipbuilding Report Reveals Navy Is Killing CG(X) Cruiser Program," *Inside the Navy*, December 7, 2009.

---

adequately with a radar smaller enough to be fitted onto the DDG-51.[68] Reports suggested that the new smaller radar would be a scaled-down version of the AMDR originally intended for the CG(X).[69]

The Navy's February 2010 report on its FY2011 30-year (FY2011-FY2040) shipbuilding plan, submitted to Congress in conjunction with the FY2011 budget, states that the 30-year plan:

> Solidifies the DoN's [Department of the Navy's] long-term plans for Large Surface Combatants by truncating the DDG 1000 program, restarting the DDG 51 production line, and continuing the Advanced Missile Defense Radar (AMDR) development efforts. Over the past year, the Navy has conducted a study that concludes a DDG 51 hull form with an AMDR suite is the most cost-effective solution to fleet air and missile defense requirements over the near to mid-term....
>
> The Navy, in consultation with OSD, conducted a Radar/Hull Study for future destroyers. The objective of the study was to provide a recommendation for the total ship system solution required to provide Integrated Air and Missile Defense (IAMD) (simultaneous ballistic missile and anti-air warfare (AAW) defense) capability while balancing affordability with capacity. As a result of the study, the Navy is proceeding with the Air and Missile Defense Radar (AMDR) program....
>
> As discussed above, the DDG 51 production line has been restarted. While all of these new-start guided missile destroyers will be delivered with some BMD capability, those procured in FY 2016 and beyond will be purpose-built with BMD as a primary mission. While there is work to be done in determining its final design, it is envisioned that this DDG 51 class variant will have upgrades to radar and computing performance with the appropriate power generation capacity and cooling required by these enhancements. These upgraded DDG 51 class ships will be modifications of the current guided missile destroyer design that combine the best emerging technologies aimed at further increasing capabilities in the IAMD arena and providing a more effective bridge between today's capability and that originally planned for the CG(X). The ships reflected in this program have been priced based on continuation of the existing DDG 51 re-start program. Having recently completed the Hull and Radar Study, the Department is embarking on the requirements definition process for these AMDR destroyers and will adjust the pricing for these ships in future reports should that prove necessary.[70]

In testimony to the House and Senate Armed Services Committees on February 24 and 25, 2010, respectively, Admiral Gary Roughead, the Chief of Naval Operations, stated:

> Integrated Air and Missile Defense (IAMD) incorporates all aspects of air defense against ballistic, anti-ship, and overland cruise missiles. IAMD is vital to the protection of our force, and it is an integral part of our core capability to deter aggression through conventional means....

---

[68] Amy Butler, "STSS Prompts Shift in CG(X) Plans," *Aerospace Daily & Defense Report*, December 11, 2009: 1-2.

[69] Cid Standifer, "NAVSEA Plans To Solicit Contracts For Air And Missile Defense Radar," *Inside the Navy*, December 28, 2009; "Navy Issues RFP For Phase II of Air And Missile Defense Radar Effort," *Defense Daily*, December 24, 2009: 4.

[70] U.S. Navy, *Report to Congress on Annual Long-Range Plan for Construction of Naval Vessels for FY 2011*, February 2010, pp. 12, 13, 19. The first reprinted paragraph, taken from page 12, also occurs on page 3 as part of the executive summary.

To address the rapid proliferation of ballistic and anti-ship missiles and deep-water submarine threats, as well as increase the capacity of our multipurpose surface ships, we restarted production of our DDG 51 Arleigh Burke Class destroyers (Flight IIA series). These ships will be the first constructed with IAMD, providing much-needed Ballistic Missile Defense (BMD) capacity to the Fleet, and they will incorporate the hull, mechanical, and electrical alterations associated with our mature DDG modernization program. We will spiral DDG 51 production to incorporate future integrated air and missile defense capabilities....

The Navy, in consultation with the Office of the Secretary of Defense, conducted a Radar/Hull Study for future surface combatants that analyzed the total ship system solution necessary to meet our IAMD requirements while balancing affordability and capacity in our surface Fleet. The study concluded that Navy should integrate the Air and Missile Defense Radar program S Band radar (AMDR-S), SPY-3 (X Band radar), and Aegis Advanced Capability Build (ACB) combat system into a DDG 51 hull. While our Radar/Hull Study indicated that both DDG 51 and DDG 1000 were able to support our preferred radar systems, leveraging the DDG 51 hull was the most affordable option. Accordingly, our FY 2011 budget cancels the next generation cruiser program due to projected high cost and risk in technology and design of this ship. I request your support as we invest in spiraling the capabilities of our DDG 51 Class from our Flight IIA Arleigh Burke ships to Flight III ships, which will be our future IAMD-capable surface combatant. We will procure the first Flight III ship in FY 2016.[71]

Author Contact Information

Ronald O'Rourke
Specialist in Naval Affairs
rorourke@crs.loc.gov, 7-7610

---

[71] Statement of Admiral Gary Roughead, Chief of Naval Operations, before the House Armed Services Committee on 24 February, 2010, pp. 10-11; and Statement of Admiral Gary Roughead, Chief of Naval Operations, before the Senate Armed Services Committee on 25 February 2010, pp. 10-11.
